THE GA
CHANGE

MY ZEN STEPS
TO UNLEASH
SUCCESS, BALANCE
AND HAPPINESS

The Change Catslyst

Dear... Preyan,

Change is the only constant in life.

I believe learning to dance with change keeps one energized and enthusiastic and makes life worth living.

I hope you enjoy reading this Book. I would love to hear your reviews.

You can also post the reviews on the Amazon website, where the books are also available, should anyone wish to order.

With lots of love and best wishes.

www.coachingwithgeeta.com
www.thegameofchange.net

First published in 2018
Copyright © 2018 Geeta Ramakrishnan

ISBN
Print: 978-0-6483402-0-1
E-book: 978-0-6483402-1-8

Because of the dynamic nature of the internet, any web addresses or links contained in this book my have changed since publication and my no longer be valid. The information in this book is based on the authors' experiences and opinions, the views expressed in this book are solely those of the author and do not necessarily reflect the views of the publisher, and the publisher herby disclaims any responsibility for them.

The author of this book does not dispense any form of medical advice, legal, financial or technical advice either directly or indirectly. The intent of the author is only to offer information of general nature to help you in your quest for personal development and/or self-help, in the event you use any of the information in this book the author and the publisher assume no responsibility for your actions. If any form of expert assistance is required, the services of a competent professional should be sought.

Publishing information

Publishing, design and production facilitated by Passionpreneur Publishing www.PassionpreneurPublishing.com

PASSIONPRENEUR
P U B L I S H I N G

Content developed using the services of the Ultimate 48 Hour Author www.48HourAuthor.me

Ultimate
48 Hr Author

Tel: 1 300 664 006
Diamond Creek
Melbourne, Victoria
Australia 3089

Testimonials

Geeta is a skilled life coach whose approach is both sensitive and supportive of the transformative process during sessions that takes you from a place of subjective reflection to positive and life-enhancing introspection. It is wonderful to heal through real conversations that are seamlessly integrated with the values of leadership, family and key relationships - conversations with a life coach who helps you navigate an increasingly complex world of new responsibilities and expectations across spaces at work and at home.

Malini N Menon
Founder and Managing Director,
IEDEA, Dubai.

Geeta has been a gift that has helped me make some much-needed positive changes in my life. Working closely with Geeta has given me the ability to step away from myself and observe my old behavior patterns that had not been serving me or those close to by. I was able to quickly identify and recognize how and why I had begun to repeat and replicate certain reactions and actions that were having a negative impact on a daily basis. I felt an instant connection to Geeta, not only was she able to guide with love and compassion, she had the instinct to nurture and push the boundaries where required. I will always be grateful to Geeta for helping me to become the best version of me.

Lucy Bruce
Co-Founder: Home Grown Children's Eco Nursery, Dubai.
Founder: Harmony House India, a charitable organization.

I met Geeta through work. We chatted and she told me about ontological coaching. I had a plethora of things 'jumbled' in my head at that time and decided to give it a try! I had a number of sessions and thought at first was unsure, I then looked forward to them and almost seamlessly my jumbled mind calmed. I was also given a breathing/relaxation exercise which I still do first thing in the morning and I just seem to be more in control... Thank you Geeta.

Dr. Barry Lynch, BDS MSc
Prosthodontist, Dubai.

Geeta's life lessons have indeed brought much inspiration to me, challenging me to break free from my attitudinal limitations and to believing in greater heights. Her coaching abilities are par excellence and I am grateful for having met her.

Vivek Vijayan
Founder: ZenQua, Dubai.
An aquascape designer who
re-aligns nature with your inner soul.

Geeta is an excellent ontological coach, helping leaders create a harmonious balance in their lives by working in a holistic manner through their work and life issues. In her calm, non-judgmental tone and by using insightful questions, she is able to effect powerful changes in individuals by helping them think through and find effective solutions for the problems they might be facing. Having experienced her ontological coaching first hand, I can safely say that she has mastered this powerful yet difficult 'art' form.

Tarun Arora
CEO: GIST, Delhi,
A leading provider of educational content.

Geeta is focused, grounded and offers good observations, insights and tools for me to introspect and prioritize. I got a different perspective to life and felt it helped me grow as a person.

Orime Fujita
CEO & President, Fujita KazuaShoten Ltd, Japan.

Sometimes we lose our inner guiding voice to the loud and needy voices of the external world; this takes us away from things that matter the most. Geeta is playing a crucial role of helping me rediscover that inner balance; she is helping me understand my goals, guiding me to find a way to get them and most importantly to keep at it. I am learning that path to redefining my life starts and ends with me; everything outside it shouldn't matter. Self-loving is self-healing. I hope to learn more from her with each session and this book.

Swati S.
PR Professional, Mumbai.

Working with Geeta has been an absolute pleasure. What I most admire in her is an unwavering and courageous commitment to her own personal growth and development. She is definitely a seeker, bringing her warmth, lightness and curiosity along, in her quest to expand herself, gain greater wisdom, and make a positive and meaningful contribution to others and the world.

Alejandra Silberman
*PCC, Somatic coach—Embodied learning
for leaders and coaches, Chile.*

Geeta has an astute ability to be fully present and yet able to hold the container for different systems in play within the coaching conversation. It was my privilege to work with her and see her grow into a confident woman and coach. She is truly a gift.

Dr. Katrina Gisbert-Tay, M.D.
Coach Supervisor and Integrative Health Coach.

Meeting with Geeta, has been an incredible experience. She plays the role of great sounding board, and also offers important inputs to trigger our thoughts. The best part of this is she empowers you through the discussions to take your life in your own hand and solve your own issues. Different perspectives to look at things, providing small milestones towards your aim, are the best takeaways from the sessions.

Manisha Mishra
HR Professional, Dubai.

I met Geeta, at a time that I needed her the most, having taken a sabbatical from work, she helped me prioritize what was important to me and guided me to focus on my hidden strengths. Geeta helped me look at a life differently.

Smita Rajeev Abraham
HR Professional, Dubai.

Have had the occasion to interact with Geeta on her recent endeavor to counsel and assist women in leadership positions to face the somewhat unique challenges they face for being a woman:

To be taken as seriously as her male counterparts
To be able to juggle and discharge multiple roles effortlessly
To be able to deal with guilt for ignoring some "natural" roles sometimes.
Found her insights very enlightening and her methods very helpful. I wish her all the very best in all her ventures.

Maya Sinha
Former IRS officer, Founder: CMC Skills Pvt Ltd
and Clear Maze Consulting Pvt Ltd, India,
focused on skill development for the underprivileged.

I dedicate this book to
My mother, Rajiamma
and my grandmother, Paru.
My husband, Ramesh.
My children Ritesh, Upasana, Anisha and Amit.
My canine companions Casper and Fivestar.

Without all your encouragement and support
I could not have been able to dance with the change
and write about it too.
Thank you for believing in me.

Acknowledgements

I wish to acknowledge the people who contributed to the making of this book. I am grateful to be blessed with good friends like you.

Ramesh Ramakrishnan of Transworld Group of Companies, Dubai; My life partner. I owe my life to you. Your constant support and encouragement helped discover a different me, a thinking, feeling and intuitive me.

Dr. K M Venkatesh, my uncle who has been a constant source of my inspiration.

My friends Radha Krishnan and Avani Shah who act as my safe sounding board where we discuss literally anything and everything under the sun. Together we form the "famous" RAGS team.

D N Prasad, PCC, a Leadership Coach who introduced me to my life changing Ontological coaching program from Newfield Asia, Singapore.

Rajesh Najgee of Chrysalis Management Institute, Dubai; who sowed the thought of book writing in my head.

Moustafa Hamwi, Passionpreneur & Chief Energy Officer, Dubai; for pushing me with passion.

Anne Hockett, Founder and MD of YouHealing International, Bali. The guided 7 days fast I did with you, cleansed my life, body and soul.

Kevin Bromley Bsc, DPodM, MSChP of Step in Time, Hertfordshire, United Kingdom; my podiatrist who thought me that your body and mind are related and can consciously change both each and every day of your life.

Dr. Kousalya Nathan of KALM Private Limited, Chennai; my wellness guide, through whom I learned of the art of cellular change, enabled with the body and mind and introduced it in my daily living.

Natasha and Stuart Denman of The Ultimate 48 Hr Author, the editor and illustrator: Richard Burian and Nikola Boskovski, Embassy Books and the publishing team, who made my dream come true.

Table of Contents

Introduction

My book is called *The Game of Change.* This book is for all the amazing women out there, in their capacity as daughters, mothers, office goers, managers, entrepreneurs, home keepers, dreamers and achievers. It is also for all the wonderful men who get to interact with these amazing women. I am writing about my experience on what worked in nurturing the power of success in the three important people of my life – my husband, my son and my daughter – without compromising mine. This subject has always intrigued me, and it has been a dream to share it in a book form to reach as many people as possible. This book is to serve all the women to unleash their potential.

Today's world is challenging and demanding. We women are handling multiple and complex roles. It ranges from being a daughter, mother, wife, daughter-in-law, mother-in-law, entrepreneur, driver for your children, office goer, manager, home keeper, mentor, caregiver, philanthropist and most often we play several of these roles simultaneously.

Along the way we have to deal with powerful men, and we want to be assertive but not seem aggressive. We want to be confident and capable in all the roles, big and small. The juggling is hard work and exhausts us. It requires a lot of patience and perseverance.

We live 99% of our lives in perceived reality. Stress is part of the norm, releasing harmful chemicals in our system which are addictive. It makes it hard to free ourselves of this repetitive pattern, making us live in anxiety and fear. It tires us and reflects on our moods, immune system and health.

We have to learn to communicate with clarity, delegate, prioritize without more drama than what we already have at hand. We are natural nurturers, and love to offer our support to others, but not at the cost of our individuality and our achievements.

Having repeatedly gone through this processes myself; as a grand-daughter, daughter, wife and life partner, mother, friend, entrepreneur and Ontological coach, this book offers my perspective on how to handle these roles efficiently and without stress. This is about being the ideal you without compromising yourself while juggling this huge task along with life's other responsibilities.

I am writing this book to serve us women. I have reflected on my experiences, offering techniques to make you more productive, successful and thrive in this complex world, with finding balance and happiness. I have shared my personal experiences which any woman can relate to, across cultures and geography. I hope to give clarity on what to change and how to change effectively.

I appreciate all the women giving so much for their family, and contributing to the society. I understand the struggle.

I do not have ready answers. As a daughter, I have a strong willed, understanding and supporting mother. However, I had to invent Geeta: a wife to an ambitious entrepreneur, mother to two amazing children, and the Geeta that is Me, nurturing my ambitions and needs. It took me 50 years to achieve my dreams and be at peace and harmony with myself and with the people around me. I persistently follow my dreams. My "I am not perfect" Mantra allows me to get more and more from life. It gives me an opportunity to change effectively into a happier person, every day. Each day I learn new things from my surroundings, sometimes from the pesky fly in my room, and sometimes from the books I read, and sometimes from the people around me.

Now as I see my daughter and daughter-in-law stepping into this chaotic world, I am emotionally invested in this cause. I do not believe you have to take 50 years to achieve this amazing transformation. To be standing on your own and be able to nurture your dreams and offer your support to the people around you. I wish to offer my experience in this book and have some easy to follow exercises at the end of each chapter.

Try it out and I will consider myself grateful if something in this book resonates with you and catalyzes a shift in your lives even in the smallest way possible. The new learning needs to be practiced over and over, at least for a few weeks, till it becomes your new habit, your new friend and a new happy you.

My chapter *Zero to Hero* talks about what it takes to move out of the "I am a victim and the whole world hates me" attitude to taking charge of your life. There is no age to change. You are looking at your biological age not the chronological age. How you breathe, what you eat and how you feel and think, all of this alters your body and mind at any age. Dr. J B Taylor, a neuroanatomist, an author and a brain stroke survivor describes us humans as 'feeling creatures that think and not thinking creatures that feel'. Your core values lead you to feel and think and create the reality around you. Dreaming and passionately following your dreams helps them to become true. So be mindful of what you dream.

Using tools like time management, being emotionally potent, your heart and head can meet at the right place, helping you breathe at the right pace and allowing your coherent best to operate. This helps to show up positively in your relationship at home and at work. You become a super human. This helps you be happy and find the Zen balance in whatever you choose to do. You realize the choice is in your hands. I follow my intuitive Yin way to achieve my dreams, with a perfect Yang balance. And yes, you can have it too.

ONE

Zero to Hero

Zero People

When was the last time you blamed someone for something?

What makes a person a zero? It is a person who's always blaming others for whatever circumstances that he or she is undergoing. Someone who feels life is always unfair and that bad things happen only to them. They don't want to take responsibility for unpleasant things and circumstances.

I would call such a person the victim. The victim is into the blame game but is oblivious of this fact. It could be because of a lack of control over the circumstance, it could be because of habitual procrastination and sometimes it is fear holding the person back. There could be so many reasons.

To give you an example...Sonia, my imaginary book friend is going to demonstrate:

It is Monday morning and the kids have basketball practice and have to be dropped to school an hour early today. The alarm rings, but Sonia hits the snooze button a couple of times. When she's finally up, she is cursing the whole world for getting up late. Her second daughter's shoe is missing, and another five minutes goes by. After what seems like a storm struck house, Sonia and her two daughters leave for school, all of them in a bad mood, not wanting to speak to each other. God, it has to be me, *she thinks, very irritated and angry. Sonia thinks she is a victim, a zero.*

Hero People

What makes a person a hero? A hero is somebody, who takes 100% responsibility for their results in life. You always stay focussed and you have faith, you don't give up easily. You believe you can achieve your dreams, you're not scared of dreaming. The irony of life is the more you believe in yourself, the more you will try. The more you try, the better the chance of you achieving it. Whether things go well or not so well, it is always your responsibility. It means that you are responsible. In your endeavor to succeed, you will try and make changes that will help you achieve what you want to get.

The benefits of being a hero

I would say one of the benefits of taking responsibility over your actions is the ability to catch yourself in an unresourceful state. To be an observer and notice what happened to you and around you. It enables you to take action, knowing what to do next. You can spend your life hating. Hating yourself, your boss who overburdened you with work, your customers as they are always nit picking, your spouse who wants his or her needs met above yours or your family for not listening to you and thanklessly making you work so hard all the time. You start to believe nobody understands you and your life are stuck and with it you are stuck too.

Challenges to being a hero

Instead of hating the situation, you can say, well this is what you have. What can you do to make it better? You can change your job, you can even change your spouse, but guess what, the likelihood of you complaining and whining and being miserable may not disappear. Once you start being responsible for at least some of your actions, you try to get hold of the situation. Even noticing what's happening around you is a good place to start. You then become open to ideas, you will intuitively know what works for you. You have to allow yourself that space to be intuitive, trust yourself rather than being burdened with negative thoughts. The best gift you can give your body is a happy liver. A happy liver means you learn forgiveness. Maybe not so much for the others than for yourself. The liver is the area in your body responsible for suppressed anger and resentment. Forgiveness lets the toxins flow out of the system and gives you the mental and physical clarity to lead a good, happy life.

Solutions to becoming a hero

Try out new things. Try and look at the problems from a different angle. The ability to see choices is very useful. Once you're out of the negative process of self-pity, you're able to rise up and see what the choices are around you and what life is offering for you. Positive thoughts help build your life skills, helping you at work and in relationships. It helps you be proactive and take positive steps. The whole round of negative, self-pity disappears.

This makes it easier to find solutions for your problem. Unless you try different solutions, you will never know if they work or not. Negative emotions such as fear and anxiety are good for protecting you, but they have a limited shelf life. Imagine that Sonia opens the door and sees a snake right there in front of her. She will instinctively scream, will get extremely anxious, slam the door shut and run away. That will be anyone's immediate fight or flight response.

However, not everything in life is a snake. If you had the chance to think clearly, you might see that what looked like a snake was actually a rope. A rope that you mistook for a snake. The chances of a snake coming to a cosmopolitan city, in the well-developed world, in your apartment, are less than 1 in 100.

Dealing with anxiety by being empathetic

Anxiety results in a loss of ability to think clearly. The ability to think comes back when you pause and take a deep breath. What is most important is that you have a choice here, to run or to pause.

When you empathize, you try and look at a situation from the other person's perspective. That is what empathy means. There is no guarantee that you've got the right perspective. Be open to the options. Empathy is the emotion that helps you connect, rather than judging the situation or determining if the other person is right or wrong. Just by understanding another person's feelings, thoughts and perspective helps you open up to possibilities.

You have the power to change. Most people wait and think the other person has to change. Rarely do you think that the change happens in you and from within you. However this thought is so powerful that it can change the other person positively.

When there is a fight or an argument, you often wonder, why can't the other person understand? Why can't he or she change? But the solution to the issues could be within you. Once you understand, with empathy, maybe you can articulate your thoughts in a way that is more acceptable to the other person, or maybe you begin to understand his or her point of view. You then realize that you have an opportunity to relook at the situation. Either way the power to change is within you.

95% of people live in a victim state. Can you imagine what that does to people in general? This impacts not just you, it impacts all the hundreds of people around you. You are constantly living in a state of blame, maybe for something big or something insignificant at some time in your life. It's going to affect the way you perceive things in a major way. This will limit your ability to see a better choice with this state of mind.

John Reyes said, "Your happiness depends on your self-reliance to take responsibility of your life, regardless of who had a hand in making it the way it is now". It is about being the hero in your life, not the victim. It is not waiting for a Superman to come and save you, but it is about you being your own Superman or Superwoman.

Many times, you don't know you are playing a victim game. You're not even aware of it, as it has become a habit, a part of who you think you are. Here are the signs you have to look for.

You constantly blame others for all your problems. It can never be you. You are the one who's stuck. Other people helping you find themselves being dragged down along with your negative drama. Your drama affects other people. They do not want to deal with people like you and you are unable to resolve life or career problems. You can also be suffering from poor relationship issues and your health may be deteriorating.

You end up taking people for granted, rather than being grateful for their help. You say things like, "Yeah, it's always like this, my life sucks, my life is always miserable". You feel it is your right, and your family has to help you because you are the victim after all.

In this negativity mode, you are unable to think about others, because you are only thinking about yourself. This is a self-destructive and selfish pattern. To get rid of these self-destructive and selfish patterns, start parking your worries on the side. They are valid and you do validate your worries and that's okay, but park them on the side for now and focus on other things. Focus on the things that work. Try helping your family by asking them what their concerns are and what you can do for them.

Help a stranger in the elevator by holding the door for him or her. Such small acts of kindness will start empowering you and will help you out of your negative victim role by giving you confidence and self-esteem. Soon your path is created from zero to hero. Help yourself to become your own hero.

"Self-pity is easily the most destructive of all narcotics. It's addictive. It gives momentary pleasure and separates the victim from reality". This is what John W. Gardner had to say. Are you a blamer? Most people who play the victim don't realize it. Sonia used to live the better part of her life as a victim. Before I got to know her, I thought that she had it all. A good house, a good family, a good business... what more could one possibly need? But as I got to know her, I was shocked to notice how much she complained about everything. Her husband travelled, and she whined about it. Her teenage children didn't listen to her and she whined. She developed hypertension and diabetes and now she whines about that too. I've known her for the past 10 years and her family has only become more prosperous, her children married well, but her whining did not stop. It ate into her health and her peace of mind and she did nothing about it, because she didn't even notice it.

Knowing how you feel on a daily basis

How do you feel on a daily basis? Are you mostly in a positive or a negative mode? Can you relate to Sonia's story? Would you rather whine and let life pass away until one day you are dead?

Or would you rather do something about it? It is not easy to come out of the whirlpool of doubt and self-pity. You can be your own Superman or Superwoman and all you need is to start noticing how this negative attitude is doing you no good and is attacking you. That itself is the beginning of change. Noticing and accepting and asking for help.

You will find a way around as long as you are willing. Is fear ruling your life? Are you paralyzed by it? Powerless? Helpless? Hopeless? Turn fear into faith! To change, you must give up something that you hold onto, like it's your comfort blanket. Maybe the blanket is old, worn and torn and does not work anymore. Is it your fear that you will not find a substitute for this negative feeling? No one will know the answer unless you're willing to try.

Maybe the blanket is not your answer and you need something else. Maybe you're looking in the wrong place to start with. Seek with an open mind. Be a hero and there are a whole lot of things that you can work on. You will soon find something that works for you.

Most people distrust everyone else around them

On average only 30% of people have a sense of general trust of other people. This means when you meet someone, there is an element of suspicion and mistrust. To convert this mistrust into trust later on, as the relationship progresses, requires extra work and a proof of trust to make it valid. Without trust it is not easy to communicate and convey your thoughts and feelings to another person. A lot of assumptions and stories get built around the conversations. An invisible wall that comes up puts some amount of stress in the relationship.

You live in an ego driven world

In this competitive world, you are trained to be aggressive and to succeed. You snooze you lose. Your focus then tends to be on your needs and your wants. You may feel, by putting another's needs before yours, your needs won't be met. Hence the element of trust is generally missing.

This emphasis builds the ego in you to grow and be stronger. You become judgmental. Your views are more important, and you feel your views are the best. The concept of co-existence is challenged. It becomes difficult to live peacefully in a relationship, in a family, at work and even in a society or in this world. Some questions might be around whether your choice is better than my choice, your needs are more important than my needs, and so on. These are just some of the challenges that one encounters in a relationship. If there is a need to give up or step down from a career growth path between a husband and wife, who will be the one to give up? Being independent or the want to be independent, especially financially, in a relationship, seems to cause some of these issues to flare up. One of you has to give up this time perhaps.

Managing the ego in your relationships with partners or friends

You cannot win all the time. Does this put you in the position of a victim? Do you blame the people around you for not being able to achieve? Do you then live in resentment? How can you rise to be a hero in this situation?

Look at the sentence in a previous paragraph, "If there is a need to give up or step down from a career growth path between a husband and wife, who will be the one to give up?" I would rephrase the sentence as, "One of you will have an opportunity to grow in a different way". Maybe you were only looking at growth in a linear manner with respect to work alone. Maybe if you let go of your office growth graph, if you are open and creative, and positive, you may come up with something else, which could be even better for you.

Take another example of living in an apartment. You have to be mindful of the neighbors and respect some rules laid out by society. You have to learn to adjust if you want to fit in. That would mean you cannot play loud music late at night, or have noisy parties, especially on week days. Maybe you have to adjust to parking space rules. If you let your ego get in the way, and bully and fight with the community manager, or be bullied and blame society in general, you will not be respected. Instead you can take a leadership role or interact with the community manager to come up with creative solutions, for car parking issues and the others.

Religion, race, or skin color has also become an excuse to get into fights with your neighbors or even with neighboring countries. Imagine one country being partitioned into two countries for political reasons. The reason for the partition may be traced to differences in culture and race. Before the politicians proposed the partition, the people of the country would be wining, dining and laughing together. The moment the country became separated, the people from the two parts have suddenly developed an animosity to each other. Acceptance and moving on with what you have helps build a peaceful life. It is also an important step to building trust.

Building trust by focussing on the other's needs

Focussing on the other person's needs is good way to building trust. When you put the other person's needs before yours, it shows you care and have the capacity to empathize. This does not mean that you are compromising yourself and then being resentful about it. When you show empathy and the care for the other person, the trust and the respect in the relationship increases. It makes you a hero. You learn to look at situations from another perspective. You become open to new ideas. This gives the space to grow in the relationship, both personally and professionally.

Being non-judgmental helps build trust. This is more difficult than it sounds. You may agree in theory that one should not be judgmental. But this is often your default mode, to judge people. You judge the person as he or she speaks and is unconsciously assessing them from your point of view. Your friend is sharing with you about a fight she had with her husband. Both of them work and when the husband comes home tired, ask if your friend could give him a hot cup of coffee as he has a bad headache. This angered the equally tired wife. Immediately you will be judging with reference to your victim state in mind. You may think your friend's husband is an insensitive man, not considering the feelings of a woman. You will be thinking and commenting to your friend, "So typical". That is definitely not useful feedback for your friend.

Hearing your friend vent her frustration could be good for her, for it is all she wanted to do in the first place. You have to give her a good ear, not provide her with the pros and especially the cons, unless she has specifically asked you to do so.

Giving your opinion, debating and arguing will alienate people. You may think you have the best solution to the situation and offer it, whether it was warranted or not. Maybe the other person feels that they are being coerced into accepting your solution? Winning an argument is of no use if it is at the cost of dissent in a relationship. Being aggressive and manipulative, even if it is for the greater good will have short term benefits. Often it is better to be kind than right.

The result of building trust helps brings less stress and less anxiety and helps bring clarity to a situation. It makes you the hero of situations, a hero in life.

Questions to ask in any relationship:

What if you are being physically abused?

Spend your energy looking for safety rather than blaming the other person. Doesn't that help? Be brave, speak out. If you're being physically abused in your own home, there are local organizations that will help you. All you need is to step out.

What if a lot of unfortunate things happen to you in your life all the time?

Think about what your mental talk is around this? What are your assumptions? What are the positive things that happened? It can even be small, something as insignificant as having beautiful eyes and being able to see. You can eat, you can walk, you can talk. Be grateful and start counting all these blessings.

Gratefulness or gratitude will help your mind be more positive and that helps you deal with the self-talk... in other words I would say it helps you with getting out of this negative talk and thinking that only unfortunate things happen in your life all the time. Yes, life is up and down, but as there are downs, there are also ups. Learn to appreciate everything that life is offering to you.

What if you suffer from anxiety or panic attacks?

Focussing on faith and love instead will really help you out. Practice some deep breathing exercises. Don't be afraid to seek help. You can also refer to the tips shared in *Chapter 11 – Finding the Balance*. I have offered some mindfulness exercises there.

Action Steps

▶▶ *Journal moments where you have played the blame game.*

▶▶ *Start verbalizing or reflecting on your emotions every night for at least three weeks until it becomes a habit.*

▶▶ *Next time you're fearful, start focussing on faith and positivity instead and see how you feel. While it is important to acknowledge your feelings, stay focussed on positive thoughts.*

Notes

TWO

No Age to Change

CHANGE IS ALL IN THE MIND AND YOU CAN CONQUER IT

I DID IT. I WON THE MARATHON!!!

Change and how your brains process change

Change is the only constant in this world. To change, you need to know what to change, why to change and what actions to take.

The minute you are born and the first breath of air hits your lungs, you cry, and the action begins. How you act depends on you. Even if you decide not to act, it is a form of action. You always have the choice to act like you always do or to change the way you act to get better results. If you don't change, you stagnate.

The brain is a muscle. Like every muscle, the brain has a memory and it needs to be exercised. Different habits use different sets of muscles in the brain. A habit is formed by using the same neural connections and pathways, making them stronger. Other parts of the body and mind recall these habits easily. A simple example of this is a baby learning to walk.

Initially the connected parts of the brain are learning this new skill called walking. Soon it becomes a habit and goes to that part of the brain where it can be recalled almost involuntarily. As an adult, you rarely think about how you walk. How does your body maintain balance, keep you standing and place one foot in front of the other. You take this function for granted, that your brain performs meticulously and with a 100% efficiency. You neither appreciate it nor have active knowledge of it while it is happening.

Forming habits by using the brain's natural abilities

This is also how habits are formed. If it works for you, then perfect. But many times, you're so oblivious to some habits that you have created or learned from childhood and that do not work in your life any more.

Looking within yourself enables you to introspect. There are various ways you can do this. One way is to outsource help and get a trained life coach or counsellor to help you progress. Meditation is equally effective, if it is guided, otherwise it requires a lot of discipline to follow through.

Guided meditation as a way to rewire your brain

There are many apps available to help you with guided meditation. Once the habit that does not work is identified, changing it is a matter of constant practice of the new habit, until it forms a strong neural pathway in your brain. The new habits you try may not work either, however you are now aware of the issue and have an opportunity to try a different, more effective habit.

Change is never easy, but science is on your side

As in most things in life, change is not easy. Results in the field of neuro plasticity find that your brain is malleable, and it is possible to enhance brain functions with specific training at any age. Your brains can change physically and functionally throughout your lifetime, with changes in your behavior, outlook, emotion and environment. Positive thinking, mindfulness and Cognitive Behavior Therapy (CBT) are some of the ways to achieve this. CBT is nothing but changing the way you think and feel to affect your behavior.

Change brings a positive outlook and enthusiasm and peace in life. Even if the circumstances around you do not change, a change in perception or belief will help you look at the same situation or problem from a different angle. You will learn to see and appreciate why you were unable to change and what was holding you back.

Allow yourself to be vulnerable and give up the fear of the unknown future. Your brain is usually in auto mode and used to following a routine. Any disruption to the pattern sends panic signals to the brain. There's a fear of the new way of thinking and being, including fear of change itself, as your brain is not used to it.

Once you look within and are able to see the distinctions, the shift happens. Practicing the new habits until they become a part of you helps you change.

Never be afraid of making mistakes; the path to success is fraught with mistakes

Mistakes help you adapt and help you achieve success. Do not be afraid to make mistakes. As you adopt change, you will see more than one way of putting things across in a conversation or getting things done. Mistakes help to point out new opportunities. Trying out new methods and thinking out of the box is a sure sign of success.

Dr. Carol Dweck of Stanford University has been studying people's mindset towards learning for decades. She found that neural connections are deepened by making mistakes and learning from them, rather than safely repeating the same task you know and feel you are good at, or think you are good at.

Empathy is a good habit that helps you grow

Empathizing is a good habit to create. Empathy is simply the ability to understand the feelings of another person by putting yourself in his or her place. It is the ability to understand how the other person thinks or feels. Empathy asks you to listen without judging, to develop and deepen your listening skills. This helps in building trust. When you listen, you hear without interfering.

Generally, people react, because they only see things from their perspective, be it in a workplace or in a relationship. With empathy, one is able to be more proactive and see the need to change from another point of view. It helps people grow as individuals.

Through empathy your relationships will blossom and have a positive effect on your health and finances. Once you are able to connect, whether in your workplace or your home, you are able to see and appreciate others' point of view, not necessarily agreeing with them. The change is natural and leads to peaceful and harmonious relationships. This has a positive impact on your health. It promotes good mental and physical health, good eating habits; good workout regimes, good sleep and even reduce stress.

There are many positive side effects of developing these challenging abilities

Once you learn to work in a peaceful environment, when there is less stress, you get more time. This increases your productivity and increases your chances of success. It also helps you see more opportunities. When you change your mindset, problems and issues become opportunities. If you are used to seeing issues in the same old way and try the same old method a hundred times and assume that the other person is going to change or understand, then you will still be stuck with the same problem.

It's natural that you may be irritated, disconnected and disgruntled. The willingness to be open and letting go of any blocks or resentments you hold introduces new energy into your system. It is that of joy and excitement and the new opportunities that come with it.

People spend 95% of their time assessing their past and thinking about the fear of future uncertainties. While it is natural to assume that persuading people and showing them facts helps them change, it has been found that people whose self-confidence and beliefs are challenged with sweeping evidence become even more stuck in their old beliefs and will not change.

George Bernard Shaw said, "Progress is impossible without change and those who cannot change their minds cannot change anything".

Some challenges you may face when making changes in your life and how to deal with them

Many times, you see and hear evidence that is contrary to your own belief system. It may kindle your interest in it for a while, but most often it is difficult to actually follow through and make the change in yourself, even if there is evidence of those things magically working. Example, a diet that leads to weight loss, but requires you to give up carbs. You will become defensive and tell yourself that you will feel weak without carbs and this diet is not for you.

Making the change is not easy. Being stuck in your own beliefs and perceptions is like a trap. You do not know how to come out of it and it begins to form a negative emotional whirlpool with it. You are skeptical about everything and fearful of what happens if it doesn't work.

The good news is you are not the only one in this situation. That is how normal brains operate. Your brain protects you from being rash and trying out things randomly. However, you need to be bold and break away from your known patterns and willing to take calculated risks and experiment a little. When you don't see how to change or think you know it all and do not want to change, you get resentful and negative. You are unable to adapt. Humans have survived through ages by adapting. That is the theory of evolution. Those who do not adapt cannot survive or succeed. Once you get trapped in the negative attitude, you lose your ability to empathize and connect. This affects your relationship at home and at work; your mind becomes stubborn. Not knowing what to change and how to change makes you lose sight of the opportunities around you.

"If you don't like something, change it. If you can't change it, change your attitude", is an apt quote from Maya Angelou.

My grandmother is in her late 90s. I have seen her grandmother, who lived to be 100. My grandmother has access to two generations of information before her and three generations after her. She is an amazing encyclopedia of information. What I like about her is her ability to adapt. In her generation, she was not allowed to come out of the kitchen when they had visitors, especially men. The women's clothes must fully cover their body. Yet when she sees her great grandchildren prancing around in modern clothes that could range from short dresses to purposefully torn jeans, she's curious and enquires about these new trending styles. She makes it a point to appreciate their clothes, the colors and how good they look on her great grandchildren.

I love her enthusiasm for life and I guess her flexibility is what makes her happy. Like Mahatma Gandhi said, "Be the change you want to see in the world".

Be flexible and open to learning new skills if you want change in your life

Be flexible and open in your approach. Do not be afraid to try new things and new ideas. Let go of your baggage, it will only pull you down. Learn new skills. It does not matter if you are young or old, it could be learning to sing, or even hum a few of your favorite songs, or even learning to play a game of Mah-jong. You will have a new way to socialize with your friends. New skills fire and activate different parts of your brain. You need not be the best at them, but it's still a new skill for your brains to learn.

Try doing things differently. Take new routes to the office. Notice the people around you, their clothes, the cars around you, the range in your car's speedometer, the trees around you, the flowers on your way as you drive, instead of thinking about your meeting and how you're going to handle a new project while you are driving.

If you are thinking about your meeting, it's like living the same moment over and over. No one can predict the precise future of what is going to happen. Imagine how many moments you missed thinking of the future and you miss the present, where you could take a long breath and just be. Observe things and be more curious. Being observant brings you to the present.

Cooking is a good mind-body exercise. The food connects your body with your mind through more than one sense. It is the touch, smell and colors of the vegetables or meat that fires up your imagination of how the meal is going to taste once it is prepared.

The science behind how breathing affects your ability to change

According to Christina Zelano, a professor of neurology at Northwestern University Feinberg School of Medicine, your breath stimulates neurons in the olfactory cortex, amygdala and hippocampus, all parts of the limbic system. These are the areas in the brain relating to emotions, memory and the centre of smell. The limbic system is related to emotion, memory and learning and controls your behavioral patterns.

How you breathe has a profound impact on the way you remember things around you. Breathing creates electric impulses in your brain that help in forming your memories, in conjunction with emotions. It has an impact on your autonomous nervous system. For example, if you have experienced something frightening, by literally holding your breath for a moment or shallow breathing, you reduce the oxygen intake, which tightens the muscles and creates tension and increases your stress. Shallow breathing tries to block the emotion, but it creates more anxiety and confusion in you.

When you are in fear, your breathing rate increases, and this is a good thing because it makes the time taken to respond to the situation faster. Your reaction is quick and instinctive, focussed on saving your life. But when you start acting in this manner to any and every stress, most of it created by you, this affects your logical and cognitive thinking ability. Breathing fast decreases the oxygen and increases the carbon dioxide in your blood stream, making the pH of the blood more acidic, which makes the muscles tighten and make you irritable and anxious.

A breathing technique to help you in a stressful situation

If you are trying to memorise something, such as when you're studying for an exam or preparing for an interview or a presentation, taking in long deep breaths while preparing can help you in this process. Training to breathe slowly and deeply helps you become more relaxed and in control of the situation. Deep breathing connects you to your coherent thinking and creative energy. Take in a long slow breath from your nostrils, to the count of four, imagining that your stomach is a balloon and you are filling it with fresh air while breathing in. Expand your chest at the same time that you expand your stomach. You can feel this process taking place by placing your right hand on your stomach, while being seated and trying the slow breathing technique. Then on the count of four, breathe the air out through your nostrils, and feel the air leaving your chest and then your stomach, totally emptying your chest cavity and your stomach.

Practicing this deep breathing technique helps you ground your thoughts. Your cognitive thinking gets enhanced. Your actions are more rational and more likely to help you in life. If you are entering a meeting, or going to face a difficult situation, a few deep slow breaths help you be calmer and get more collected. The technique increases the intake of oxygen and calms the parasympathetic nervous system.

You can test your breathing pattern by simply holding your finger below both nostrils and noticing where you are breathing out from. When the breath comes out from the left nostril, it indicates your cognitive self is engaged. Ofcourse, this pattern keeps changing naturally throughout the day. Conscious deep breathing can make you breath out more from you left nostril.

How often to practice this breathing technique

The practice of this deep slow breathing, at least 10 minutes in the morning and 10 minutes in the evening, helps you become more aware in tune with your cognitive self.

You can practice this breathing at any age. You don't have to be young to practice it. It is an easy method, achievable by the young and old alike. You just need willpower, discipline and focus to keep practicing such breathing until it comes to you naturally and you're not thinking about it, much like the act of walking or riding a bicycle. At some point it just becomes part of your autonomous nervous system, the nervous system that controls involuntary functions of the body. Remember that most people breathe with shallow breaths by default, with hardly any change in the chest cavity let alone the stomach. At first this deep breathing might seem different to practice, but when you get used to it the long term benefits are very helpful.

This type of breathing helps you to be more alert and aids you in any change you want for yourself. While old age could dull your memory, practicing this breathing can give you an opportunity to improve your memory under the given circumstance. The cognitive mind, aided by this breathing practice allows you to learn new skills. These skills can be physical activity or a mental activity. You can learn to run a marathon even when you are in your 80s or older. Fauja Singh is a British national of Indian origin. He is about 100 years old. He used to participate in running races when he was young. He got so busy with life, he had forgotten this passion of his. In his late 80s he rekindled his passion for running marathons. When he was 93 he completed a 26.2 mile marathon, 58 minutes better than the last world record in the 90s-age group.

Meditation is not a complex skill which can only be achieved by a few. One tends to perceive it as something mystical for hermits or gurus. While society gives less importance to spiritual knowledge, access to techniques from such ancient routes can help with daily success in your lives.

Meditation does not mean that you have to sit cross legged on the floor. The process of slowing your breath and observing your thoughts come and go is a form of meditation in itself. You can practice this comfortably by sitting in a chair, keeping your back as straight as possible, and observing your breath and thoughts. Image the possibilities that open up. Imagine being able to just listen to people talk, no matter how they make you feel or what you think of and just being a reassuring presence for them. Stress is known to promote high blood pressure and bad blood cholesterol, and cause Alzheimer's in your advanced age. But you can beat Alzheimer's. Keeping your mind active with various brain gym activities like Sudoku and other games that improve hand-eye coordination, as well as memory games can also help. Practicing such mind games with deep breathing and meditation will keep your mind young and active, with an ability to learn as much if not more than a young adult.

Questions to ask related to breathing and your biology:

What if you know that having sweets makes you put on weight, yet you cannot resist it. How do you change to healthy eating?

Often the problem lies elsewhere. Dig deeper. Most of us eat emotionally. The overeating issue is related to some other emotional problem. Eating sugar and carbs gives short term relief for these emotional issues. Emotional eating is a real problem and needs to be addressed.

What if you are afraid to try and it seems like too much of a risk?

Fear is an essential part of survival. You need fear to protect you, but when you are controlled by fear, that becomes a problem. Accepting fear will allow you to try change and take calculated risks, helping you to take one baby step at a time.

What if you have tried to go to the gym regularly, but never succeeded for more than one month?

Change is not easy. One needs to be diligent and keep trying. It is okay if you are lazy for a day or two. Just notice it. You don't have to punish yourself for it but pick up from where you left off. Set a one-month goal and review it weekly. At the end of one month, set the next month's goal. The results excite your brains to perform. I find that committing and paying a 6-month package to your gym trainer is a good motivator and helps you continue with your gym program.

Action Steps

- *Brush your teeth with the hand other than the one you are used to.*

- *Learn a new language.*

- *Yoga is a good mind-body exercise that helps you on multiple levels in gaining discipline to mindfulness.*

Notes

THREE

Inner Urge

NURTURE VALUES AND REAP SUCCESS

Your personal value system

Look within and unleash your inner potential if you want to grow. Growth happens from the inside out.

A value system is a person's standard of what is right and wrong. This is based on your knowledge and wisdom along with your willingness to conform to these self set standards. This set of principles comes from within, forming the individual's core value and belief system. It guides you to prioritize and focus on your goals. Your values could be built around yourself, your health, your family, your work, your community, your country and around our planet earth.

Spending time defining your personal values brings an inner strength and acts as your backbone to life. You become happy, motivated and focussed towards achieving your goals in life. Appreciation, gratitude, compassion, empathy, forgiveness, respect and love are some examples of values that people have. Different people can have different sets of values. There is no right or wrong set of values. Your values need not be the same as another person. Acceptance of another's values is important and with the understanding that their values work for them as yours do for you.

Values inspire actions and influence your behavior. What are your core beliefs? What are the principles you stand for, especially when you're under pressure? How you think, and act are guided by these basic beliefs.

Values are like a rudder to a ship. They give a direction for your thoughts, words and actions. Together, it helps build a great community, where individuals are able to contribute and help each other. Values are not restricted to individuals. You can have group values. What are your values when it comes to your community or your country? If you respect nature for example, you may contribute by being part of the 'Go Green' or 'Save the Tiger' projects. There are plenty of opportunities out there to live your values.

The benefits of having a strong set of values

You build your image around your values. Good values help you gain trust from other people. You have to be sincere and believe in your values for another person to be able to resonate with those values. If mutual respect is one of your core values, then you'll be able to respect the other person's thoughts and feelings, and this helps to build a healthier relationship. You can communicate your thoughts effortlessly to the other person and be okay and accepting of another point of view.

It also helps for the other person to accept your ideas more easily and you don't have to sound like you're imposing your ideas on them. This shows up in organizational performance. A good sale happens when you are a good listener. When you have a conversation, listen to the needs of the other person before you offer your product. You soon create a bond of trust. The trust helps you seal the contract. You might have to build that trust over several conversations, but that's what helps you. Living with high values transfers to your positive performance and builds your self-esteem and confidence.

If your core values are not in sync with that of the organization, there may be conflict, affecting your growth. This also happens in a relationship.

What are your joint values in a relationship, for example? Do you have a core value that you and your partner uphold? Have you invested some time to discuss this? These are some useful points to think about. Living up to your value is a good trait to pass onto the next generation. You make hundreds of decisions daily based on your core value system.

It helps in your relationship with your family and friends. It helps in your financial and organizational growth. It then reflects in the wellness of your community and this earth as a whole. Living by example and seeing your growth and success is the best way for the younger generation to emulate the values.

Since statistics show that most people have a general lack of trust in other people, if you want to be respected by others, you can start by respecting yourself. "Only by self-respect will you compel others to respect you", is a quote by Fyodor Dostoyevsky.

Looking at your core beliefs in detail

What happens if your core belief is not stable? If it is flexible according to the circumstances, your thoughts and actions will not conform to any particular value system. People cannot trust you. Your decision will be impulsive and based on getting instant gratification. Impulsive decisions can have lifelong repercussions. There will be no solid, long term plans and goals. You will be perceived as irresponsible in your work front and in relationships, if you don't truly believe in how you project yourself to the world.

You cannot forget that the other person dealing with you may be equally intelligent and is able to grasp your intent. You lose your self-respect. Compromising your life with short term benefits consumes and destroys you. It may make you money, but you will not be happy. If you're a leader, how you show up affects your team. You will not be able to contribute to your organization and you will appear selfish and unscrupulous. There are no long term career growth opportunities. The relationship suffers when you do not have anything solid to offer. You'll have nothing much to contribute to your children's personal growth either. Eventually you become a taker from this earth, not able to contribute to yourself or the society. There is no self-worth in this equation.

This reminds me of a quote from the 14th Dalai Lama, "Open your arms to change, but do not let go of your values". You have to take on change and make a decision about yourself, your health, your finances, your relationships and your social life. Have a strategy in life. Being pushed around in your life by an overwhelming schedule, without giving it any thought, is like a rudderless ship floating aimlessly. Assign "me time" to give a lot of thought to what core values and principles you'll be operating your life on. Dial a friend for help or reflection. This investment of time forms a base of how you think and act.

Sharing your values with others in the world

What value is of most importance to you? What thoughts and actions does it generate? Do you have a vision in life? What do you hate most and don't want or like to compromise on? Have you helped your children to develop a good value system? How do you develop a good value system in children?

Start young. You cannot teach children certain things, but they learn from example. Be a good role model for them and help your children by introducing values early in life. Values such as honesty, being considerate, being respectful to elders and forgiveness.

Use stories to explain the concepts to them. Have a set of family values. Co create values with your children to get them involved and review them monthly. Form a club in your society or community, be a leader. Pick up a couple of social issues, debate them with the team members, work towards a goal and draw up an action plan. For example, create a plan to recycle clothes, get your children and the children of the neighborhood involved as well. Take up some other social cause like the fight against child labor and make a difference in society. The creation of this awareness not only changes your own image of yourself but it does so for others as well.

Many people find values in material things

You spend your life taking care of yourself. It's all about your needs, your wants, what you want from life, what you want to eat, and what you want to wear. Anything that goes against what you like makes you unhappy. Think about it for a minute. Does it apply to you? Does it apply to your family life and in your work life? With all the pressure to be achievers, you want that promotion, you want the best for your children, you want the best for your spouse, you want that luxurious dream house, the dream car… the list goes on. There is a lot of competition in life and you want the best. This process is a stressful one. Even if you have technological support to help you in life, does it really work? Watching a television program is more complex than it ever was (at least for me). Now there are 100 more choices, so what do I watch? I spend a while browsing for the best fit. The television itself is more complex to operate, it is connected to my home automation system and to the Wi-Fi. I loved the time when all I had to do was click a button and the channel appeared.

The more you surround yourself with material things, the more stressful life becomes. You need to choose what dress to wear, what food to eat and so on. It is the easy availability and the multitude of choices that makes life more difficult. Some amount of stress is good for you as it dissuades procrastination and keeps you motivated to achieve in life. There are so many distractions in life today that you need to be mindful and learn to take a pause and be the one really making the choices.

Get connected and change the energy

The irony of life is that the more you care and give, the more you reap the benefits. Be empathetic and connected through your feelings. Instead of assuming you know what works best for your teenage children, try asking them what they might want. If you think they have to be prepared to deal with this competitive world, you may want to teach them to fight and be aggressive lest they become losers. You fight for your promotion in the office, perhaps compromising a small part of your values. You want to be an equal partner in marriage, so you cannot give in all the time. Are these attitudes helping you in the long run? What does it take for you to be assertive instead? Taking that well needed pause, taking a long deep breath, listening to what the other person wants or is trying to convey, believing in yourself, being positive and open minded. Being empathetic gives you an opportunity to hear another point of view. It is an opportunity to come up with a new way of doing things, one that is less stressful, with a lighter atmosphere around it and perhaps showing better results. It changes the energy and things become less of a struggle and less of a fight. The change gives you the emotional agility to handle any situation with ease and allows your brain to be more creative and cognitive in its function. It leads to better success in life.

When you care and check in with others on their perspective, while you need not agree with them, you are connecting with them. It is better to be kind than correct. If your friend comes to you with a request that is difficult for you to fulfill, it may be a better option for you to check out what he or she has in mind, and the other choices available rather than just going straight to "no". If you have to eventually say a no, it becomes more acceptable.

Money and how it's related to happiness

Many studies show that money does not buy happiness. Yes, you need money, but not at the cost of happiness. Values that you live, shape the way you think and act. You have to believe in the values. There are no short cuts, or you cannot say that "today I am giving my values a break". When you are in business, you cannot have one value for your home, one for your children and one for your business. If your business growth involves cheating the government, you are answerable to yourself first. Can you sleep at night, living with that thought? There will be a time for payback. Have you assessed the situation? Are you prepared for the payback? Or are you short sighted and focussed on your immediate growth. Whatever you do in life, good and bad comes with consequences. What gives you happiness and a better quality of life? Is yours a life where you can care and share your thoughts, your feelings, your resources, a life in a society which makes you feel wanted and needed and a part of it. The sense of belonging and the feeling you get when can contribute to someone else's happiness and progress is worth all the money in the world.

Questions to ask related to your values

What if sometimes you have to tell white lies and compromise? Isn't it easier? One has to be practical and smart in life. Don't you think so?

Sticking to your values may not be easy, but at the end of the day you are answerable to yourself. Compromising once leads you to do it more and more and soon looking for short term gains makes you lose focus. It results in not believing in yourself and low self-esteem and no real growth. You may soon start playing the blame game and don't want to take responsibility for your life.

What if children don't listen to you?

Children learn from their parents. If you are angry they pick up anger. If you're compassionate, they learn compassion. Of course, set their limits and boundaries and explain to them why you do so. Also make sure they're aware of the consequences of crossing the limits and set silly and light punishments, such as missing their favorite half hour TV program. Follow through with the punishments. If you're willing to listen to them and give them that time to offer explanations to clarify their thoughts and be willing to forgive them and give them another chance, those are the values they will pick up.

What if you have never given a thought to what your core values are, you just live by the day?

Don't worry, you're one amongst the many. One often lives life without any thought, or should I say life lives you? Values give a focus and a game plan. They help you come up with a vision. To succeed in life, one needs a goal and a vision. You need to take time off from your daily routine. Take a pause, take a one-day break and give this some careful thought. Take the value of perseverance for example. It creates a new distinction in your goal. Discipline and will power are tools for success. Integrity is another amazing value. It helps you be strong, true to yourself and develop your inner strength.

Action Steps

▶▶ *Articulating your values now and again helps you live them.*

▶▶ *Enroll others and contribute to society. Be a leader. Take action.*

▶▶ *Teach children the value system by example. Explain in a fun way through stories.*

Notes

FOUR

Unlocking Success

Visualizing your dream

Goals are simply nothing but your dreams and ambitions put into an action plan. My father-in-law used to say that results are directly proportional to the effort. My father-in-law was a visionary. Ironically, he had only 20% vision in one eye and zero in the other. He came from a small town in South India doing a small job in a small office. He dared to dream. His dream was to own a ship and with hard work, resilience and perseverance, his dream became true.

It was not easy and definitely not for the faint hearted, but very much real and achievable. He had to give up on something to get something. He relocated to a foreign country but was unable to take his family into the uncertain future. He believed in himself and his dreams. He shared his dream with his family by making them a part of his dream and asking for their support and feedback.

He was not afraid to share his failures with his family. His core values were compassion and empathy. He introspected on his failures and learned from them. All this formed the backbone in achieving his goals. This made his family motivate him and they were with him in his journey, which was initially filled with hardship.

This motivation encouraged him to succeed. Today his children and grandchildren bear the fruits of his success. They continue to learn from him and be motivated with his success story.

How to dream big

Dream big and write it down. Dreaming what you want is an important part of goal setting. You can achieve a big, challenging goal by cutting it into smaller measurable goals. A well defined goal gives you an end point in mind. Something to work towards. Don't be too harsh on yourself if you fail. There's no shame in failure. Each failure teaches you what did not work, and it is good to invest some time in this area. It is worth evaluating the reasons for failure and to try out different ways towards the same goal. There are no ready answers nor are the answers right or wrong. Follow your intuition. Work with a broad framework, which could be your tipping point, beyond which you may have to reset the goal itself.

You may have hundreds of items on your to do list and they clutter your mind. A well thought out goal creates focus and clarity. Investing some time to develop it is a good idea. Prioritize. Once your goal is set in your mind, adding a timeline chart makes it measurable and achievable. You become accountable to the goal. It need not be overly ambitious. Something that makes you go beyond your comfort zone but you can still achieve. To achieve something, you have to push yourself a little and it may not be easy. But visualizing the end in mind and then achieving it makes it worth all the effort.

Reviewing your goals every week or every quarter helps you keep focus on your one big goal and keeps the pressure on it. Soon you become better at performing and achieving the smaller goals, until it becomes a habit. Once a habit, it goes into auto pilot mode in your brain and your brain will have more space to take up another new project, another new goal.

Making small measurable goals in the beginning helps you gain confidence and boosts your self-esteem. This helps you overcome barriers and soon you are ready for the bigger goals.

Goal setting makes demands on your discipline and your willpower. Self-discipline and willpower are useful tools to success. It does not mean being harsh and punishing yourself if you don't achieve them. It builds resilience and the inner strength to handle failures and builds your confidence. It is the perfect antidote for procrastination and helps you become an achiever. Once you taste success, it becomes addictive and you crave for more.

Related to the above, less than 10% of people stick to their New Year's resolutions. "If you want to be happy, set a goal that commands your thoughts, liberates your energy and inspires your hope", said Andrew Carnegie.

Overwhelmed by life and being busy

You get so busy with life that it consumes you. Most of you are following the small mundane, day to day and have to do lists that you don't tend to give importance to. You do not think of any short term goals, let alone long term goals.

As a child, you have so many dreams and you're not afraid. What happened as you grew older and are handling more responsibilities? Your dreams got killed. It may be as small as going for a moonlight stroll in the beach, to wanting to own a billion-dollar business. A missed opportunity gives rise to resentment and that's all you'll get.

There will be no purpose or clarity in your life, and life will go on. Procrastination, a lack of discipline and a lack of willpower are some of the evils in this game. The blame game is the easiest route to take. People who blame look for the smallest things to pass the blame onto. It creates a strong whirlpool of emotions going down the bottomless pit. You will be saying things like, the whole world is working against me, or why do all these things happen only to me? Remember Sonia? People like Sonia tend to become sarcastic and negative. Without any goal, you are lost in the day to day living.

It affects your confidence. There will be a conflict in your workplace where the yearly goals that are given to you do not match or measure to your goals and standard of work. You'll be stuck in resentment, unable to focus or achieve. It slowly becomes a habit, which eventually becomes transparent to you and you will be unable to pull yourself out of the mundane, daily work.

Oliver Wendell Holmes said, "The great things in this world are not so much where we are, but in what direction we are moving". I've found taking baby steps helps. Think and write down your big, challenging goals. Split it further into smaller, measurable and achievable goals and setting a time bar to get them, helps you achieve it.

It is less overwhelming. Once you start achieving the smaller goals, taking the next step becomes easier. Your confidence level is boosted. Take some time to brainstorm to reach a well defined goal. Use the power of visualization. You can take a picture of your goal or what you want to achieve and stick it in your bathroom mirror or the inner part of your wardrobe door.

You have five senses: touch, smell, taste, sight and sound. Associating what you want to achieve with multiple senses in your brain creates a stronger bond in your brain, giving the chance to recall it faster and to achieve it much greater.

If you want to be the best salesperson in your company, which deals in selling furniture for example, think of what success feels like to you. Picture yourself standing with a big smile of success next to your dream living room, painted in your favorite sugar cookie off-white color, with some antique furniture which the company has gifted to you as a perk. You have decorated the living room in different shades of coral and turquoise. Smell the candle and the potpourri that are on the centre table. Or think of the Bali vacation you have always dreamed of and your company has gifted to you as a reward. Imagine taking your family to Bali. Imagine the colors, the smell, the feel of seawater on your face, the greens, the yummy Balinese food. You can post a picture of Bali in your cupboard or wardrobe. Every time you see this picture, the feeling you associated with this image comes into your mind and this encourages and pushes you to perform better, helping you reach your goals in a positive frame of mind.

Make your goals measurable and articulate your goals and declare them to your friends and family. Ask for their help to check on you. This makes you more accountable for your goals. It reduces your chances for failure. Reward yourself at the end of each, small, achievable step. It could be treating yourself to a cupcake in your favorite coffee shop or taking a leisurely walk with your dog in the park or treating yourself to a nail salon date. Brains love rewards and work well with a reward system, so why not use this technique?

The science behind change

Epigenetics is the new and fast developing field of study in the changes and adjustments of gene expression caused by external, environmental factors and perception, without changing the DNA itself. This means the genes are also affected by environmental factors and changing them, without changing the DNA, could change the physical and mental state of the person. This means inheritance need not happen only through the DNA code.

The body has about 25,000 genes. What you eat, how you exercise and sleep, for example, can causes changes in the way your genes express themselves. They become either activated or inactivated. This could mean that by altering the external or environmental factors, there is a possibility of retaining some productive genetic effects and some unproductive effects like auto immune diseases and cancer can be eliminated. These traits can either be passed or not passed in a controlled manner to your next generation. The study of epigenetics, though still in the initial stages, offers such interesting possibilities. It can play a big role in evolutionary success.

The study of Kenyan house sparrows, or *Passer domesticus*, by research scientist Andrea Liebl from the University of Florida, showed epigenetic modification and adaptation capability. Studies in epigenetics show how environment and lifestyle changes are passed to the next generation. For example, children born during the Dutch famine (1944-45) have higher rates of developing coronary heart diseases. Epigenetics is a developing science and by altering the environment, one can induce positive changes to be passed on to the next generation.

The food you eat causes every cell in your body to change. Stress causes epigenetic changes. Stress causes you to adopt poor eating habits, with a tendency towards binge eating, eating the wrong type of foods. The reason can be physical deficiencies in your body to psychological use of comfort food. Epigenetics says that genes can be influenced by behavior and environmental changes. Controlling the type of food and what you eat and how you eat can influence the epigenetic markers in a positive way. Avoiding gluten, lactose, and adding healthy vegetables and fruits such as broccoli and blueberry, modifying the fat you take, all of these can have an influence on your physical and mental health.

Sugar is a good example. A study on the effect of sugar on the body showed some interesting results. Glycolysis is the process of your body breaking down sugar into energy. The extra glucose in the body is then stored as fat. If the supply of glucose is stopped or greatly reduced when you switch to a low carb diet, the body tries to get its energy from the stored fat in a process called ketosis. The body gets a message that food is being rationed (which is why it's often called "starvation mode", but you're not actually starving) and the cells of your body make the adjustments to accommodate of this lack of sugar. This is known to cause weight loss, which may not be necessarily healthy. Ketosis has its pros and cons and related diets must be practiced under medical supervision, especially if you have certain medical conditions such as diabetes or epilepsy.

Cutting calories, under a supervised diet plan, have also been shown to cause anti-aging and increase life span. The discovery of an epigenetic enzyme which is involved in fat cell transformation and its regulation through a well balanced diet can help put the process of aging on hold.

The understanding behind some peptides, which are a type of protein in the genes has been a great breakthrough in skincare. This is a result of work in the human genome field.

Mitochondria are your energy power cells. Their production slows down with age. Scientists have produced a supplement to work on the mitochondria to produce energy, thereby claiming to help you to be physically and mentally fit and younger.

According to Zachary Kaminsky, a professor of Psychiatry and Behavioral Science, while a small amount of alcohol is good for the heart, alcohol abuse affects the liver and heart, and changes its ability to process cholesterol. Exercise is known to have a positive impact on blood Cholesterol levels.

Your muscles remember exercise in the form of epigenetic markers on the DNA. While it may take a while for the muscles to get back into shape after a gym break, this muscle memory helps the process faster than you can imagine. Some studies show that exercise could epigenetically improve your physical and mental ability and help in weight loss and reduce stress. Exercise releases happy chemicals in your body and helps in not only keeping your muscles and internal organs fit, but it also helps keep you mentally fit. Any health issues negatively affect your relationships, your finances and your chances of success. It is the same with the mind. A stressed mind or a preoccupied mind worrying about the future or brooding about the past will be unable to produce good results in the present. A healthy body and mind is needed to succeed in life.

Questions to ask about your goals and change in your life:

What if you start thinking of one big goal but get completely overwhelmed?

It is good to have a vision in mind. That big goal could be your long term goal. To achieve it, what steps do you need to do today? In this month and in the next quarter? Once you cut it into smaller portions, it is not so daunting. Separate and prioritize the "have to dos" and the "must dos" and what is urgent and what can wait. Then it becomes achievable. When you evaluate regularly and notice that you did not reach the goal, you can easily introspect, and it makes it much easier to correct and fine tune your methods.

What if you are so caught up with your daily affairs that you cannot find time to think and dream? What if dreaming seems like a luxury to you?

"Outsource what you are not good at" is my mantra. There are so many competing coaches and work-life-balance gurus out there. Seek their help. You can also rope in a friend, offer to buy him or her a meal and have a chat. You can use self-help and organizing apps available everywhere including your Smartphone.

What if you are afraid you will fail? What if you will then lose what you have and also lose what you were dreaming of and didn't have it anyway?

One thing in this life is clear. You have to give up something to achieve something else. This also means drawing up a broad framework within which you will work. Push your limits, yes, but be brave to recognize when to stop.

A school girl dreaming of getting a gold medal for her school could be giving up on her sleep, her playtime and even study time as a young, aspiring swimmer. She dreams of competing for her country. What if she tried her best and didn't make it? Think of what she has gained. The training has given her discipline, resilience and a strong will.

Her brain has learned this as a habit. These are exactly the techniques she will need to grow and flourish in life. Maybe she did not become the best swimmer of her school or the country but think of the opportunities and advantages that are now open to her with the tools she built up and which her fellow students didn't. Fear and doubt only promotes failure. Be vulnerable and open yourself to succeed.

Action Steps

▶▶ *Dream big. Invest time in seeking the help of your family or friends or outsource help to formulate your big goals in life.*

▶▶ *Follow through. Evaluating your success on a weekly, monthly, quarterly basis and reviewing it annually helps.*

▶▶ *Prioritize. Make four quadrants of your "to do" list with your goals in mind.*

▶▶ *Divide them into:*

1. *Important and urgent: Do it now.*

2. *Urgent, but not important: Try and outsource help here.*

3. *Important, but not urgent: Decide on putting a date to these so that you don't procrastinate.*

4. *Not important and not urgent: These are things you can do at your leisure.*

Notes

FIVE

Beyond Overwhelm

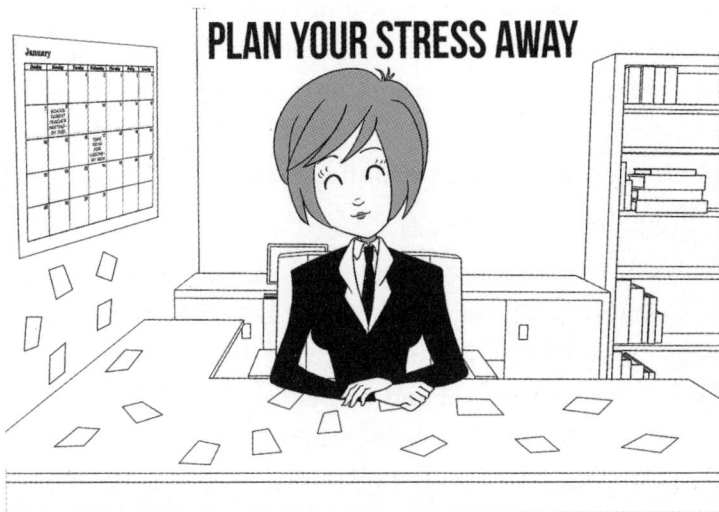

PLAN YOUR STRESS AWAY

What is time management?

I got up a few minutes late, still tired from yesterday. I look in the mirror. Now I have a bad hair day too! Just what I needed to make it worse. Ofcourse it is today that my car decided to break down and I'm late for dropping off the kids to school. I am also late for an important meeting. Sounds familiar?

In the 19th century, with the Industrial Revolution, the term "Time Management" was born. It refers to the development of the processes and tools that increase efficiency and productivity, which then translates to a business profit.

Today this has a broader perspective. It refers to a particular skill set in an individual. It has become more of a survival or a life skill and indicates how effectively one can use his or her time to be efficient. Time management is a useful skill to have, which increases your productivity in a job, what you focus on or in any thing that you choose to do.

It goes a long way in boosting your self-esteem. One needs discipline and time management is on the opposite spectrum of procrastination. It means you need to be organized and follow through with the process that is a price to pay to be and feel confident and capable in all your multiple roles.

This skill leads to less stress at work and at home, and applies to any area you choose to practice it. Less stress means there is less negative energy, and more productive energy. This leads to better physical and mental health and an increase in self-confidence. Personally, when I'm stressed, I cannot think straight, and I cannot offer my presence to my spouse or my children or to any one at work. On the contrary, I confuse myself and all those who need me.

Can you perform more tasks in the same given time and with more accuracy? Yes, that's what time management does for you. It improves and boosts your productivity. Once you allot time for set tasks during the day, you just go by your day smoothly and you know what to do and when to do it. Your day becomes more productive and makes you happier. It actually gives you more free time to pursue your hobbies and things that you love, but never thought you could do instead of being busy doing things without any structure in your day.

You get more learning opportunities and it helps you develop yourself. It helps you fine tune and update your skills and pursue higher things of interest. It offers more opportunity for career success, personal success and financial rewards as well.

Introspect the procrastination

You get more time to introspect when you manage your time. Plan your entire week on Sunday, for example. You can then allot some time, even as little as ten minutes, before you go to sleep, to introspect on the day and see how the planning worked for you. At this time you could also think of the next day and prioritize your tasks by the day and eliminate procrastination.

Interruptions are the biggest waste of time, whether it is checking social media updates on apps such as WhatsApp or Facebook, or playing games on your smart phones, or checking email every other minute, or even indulging in non-productive and negative conversations, during the umpteen numbers of teas and coffee breaks that you can take.

The average person will spend more than five years of their lives on social media according to a 2017 research survey. No wonder the advertising investment in social media amounted to around 36 billion dollars globally in that year.

To quote Albert Einstein: "When a man sits with a pretty girl for an hour, it seems like a minute. But let him sit on a hot stove for a minute, then it's longer than an hour. That's relativity".

Are you often confused, feeling stressed, finding that it leads to poor performance and productivity? All your daily tasks impact your personal and professional life. If you perform tasks under stress, it leads to more errors and soon self-doubt regarding your ability to perform creeps in. This takes a toll on your physical and mental health. You'll have no time for yourself, no time for the hobbies you always wanted to do. Things you like to do will remain in the "wanting to do" box.

The self-neglect leads to lack of confidence and you not being able to offer support to yourself, your team members or members of your household.

What happens if you are unable to prioritise or say "no"? It is very difficult to say no to others. You start accepting other people's tasks, they will learn that you are an easy target and will tend to dump all their work on you, especially the kind that is hard to deal with.

If you cannot learn to say no, it shows that you do not consider yourself important enough and you do not respect yourself enough. It shows you are weak. But you may not think so and would rather be building your own story and assumption in your head that by saying that you love to help others and that you're very kind at heart. It is, however, at your cost and your performance. Is that what you want?

It will eventually lead to resentment, lost opportunities, an inability to grow in your career with no financial success.

"The future is something which everyone reaches at the rate of 60 minutes an hour, whatever he does or whoever he is", said C. S. Lewis.

Time is relative. If you're busy and you enjoy doing what you're doing, then the whole day goes by like a breeze. If you're stressed, and struggling to do your job, while also juggling to do other people's jobs which you have unwittingly accepted, you start becoming a procrastinator and your end result will be poor.

Are you a procrastinator? I thought I was very well organized and used to finish most of my work on time. But wait, I said, "most". I then realized my focus was only on the jobs I liked to do and enjoy doing. This was irrespective of whether it was a "have to do" job or a "must do" job, or a job of no particular value. In my mind, I used to prioritize them as per my likes, pushing the ones that were important or that were difficult, or the ones I feared, to the bottom of my list.

There were some days I used to just do jobs to appear busy. I would happily procrastinate on the important ones until it was the last minute. I started forgetting important office deadlines, parent-teacher meetings, which I then used to urgently prioritize with poor distinctions on the "must do" and "have to do" job lists. This totally stressed me out. I noticed I was not able to achieve as much as I would have liked to in life, and was blaming everyone and everything around me, until one day it hit me. It forced me to reconsider what is important for me now. What I need to keep and what I need to let go.

To manage time effectively, I started devoting an hour or two every weekend and painfully organizing, structuring and prioritizing the week and the month ahead. The children's schedule, "me time" schedule, my work schedule and my social schedule. Every morning I got up 10 minutes earlier than I used to, spending the time running over my daily schedule. What worked? You can divide things into four boxes, important and urgent, most important but not urgent, not important but urgent, not important and not urgent.

Then prioritize things. People spend approximately 20% of an average working day in urgent and important matters and the remaining 80% of their time in the other three boxes. That offers barely any value to the time spent.

Following up on processes soon saved me more time for myself. My efficiency in the office increased, I was more relaxed at home, I do not remember missing any parent-teacher meetings ever again.

Stress and time management

Stress is defined as an emotional state of mind derived from a demanding circumstance or circumstances. Most often you associate and blame your circumstances and surroundings for your stress. Stress is a natural reaction of your body and is there for a reason. Stress helps the body and mind cope with the circumstance, by putting your mind in a fight or flight mode. This protects you by allowing the mind to take quick decisions.

Nowadays, life with all its amenities and gadgets ironically keeps you under constant stress. The need for achievement, professionally and financially is seen as more important than being happy and content in life. So instead of pacing life comfortably and having the ability to enjoy the smaller pleasures in life, you tend to be focussed on achieving professional laurels and financial wealth. Financial needs are unfortunately limitless. If you ask the grocer, he needs money to clear his debts, to send his children to school, to buy the car and so on. If you ask a millionaire, his answer will not be very different. Both are so caught up in day to day living that there is no space for thinking outside the day to day activities of life. Life becomes mundane, miserable and stressful that you do not know how to get out of this cycle of pressure. People blame external factors such as work-life pressure, their tyrannical boss, deadlines, competing commitments and so on for their high anxiety levels. They then validate their assessment with hundreds of facts, all of which are stories that they have built over the years, around their lives. If you're in this situation, you might have added to the complication by living in the past with regret or resentment, especially about events that you cannot change or events that can be changed, but you would rather not take that risk. Or you spend time worrying about the future, in a "what if this happens" and "what if that happens", analyzing mode, while actually no one can predict the future. Infact with your strongly negative attitude, you will unconsciously or subconsciously be creating an atmosphere to fail.

Stress only increases the chances of coronary diseases and lowers your body's immunity. Stress has not shown any ability to solve problems. Your life goes on, day after day in a dazed state. You don't notice small details around you. You are unaware of where you parked your car, or what you had for dinner last night. You miss parts of conversations, lost in a train of your own thoughts.

Looking inward allows you to reflect on many opportunities you can move forward with. You can do this with lightness. Practicing deep slow breathing with your nostrils helps you bring your attention to the present. Sometimes when your mind is drifting, or there is a possibility of a stressful situation developing, just get up, take a moment to go for a walk, shake yourself out, come back and sit down. This break allows your brain the opportunity to ground itself and access its cognitive sections. Slow breathing helps you take charge of the situation and your life. What can you do to make your life better? You can breathe and take a step back. This will give your brain time to recollect itself and introspect. This will help you make focussed and value based decisions. This will help you plan and chart a clear path for you, organizing the details in a simple doable structure. It will give you the ability to feel and connect to the situation and the people around you.

Being in the moment allows your brain to reveal its cognitive ability to resolve problems and issues in life. Once you stop the blame game and look at yourself for answers, you start being response-able. You will realize the way you see life and the stories you build in your head is what can change. Once you change, you adopt an openness that lets the people around you change. You learn to forgive, to let go, to adapt, and learn creative solutions for your issues, while being respectful of people around you. This change is powerful. I remember every morning before school was always stressful, with the "wake up, get ready, get to school on time" routine. I used to wake up expecting chaos at home and that is what I got. In hindsight, had I been more recollected and calm, I can see numerous things I could have done to make the school going experience a more pleasant one. I was super stressed and definitely not in charge, and my family recognized and mirrored the energy and made it worse.

Pausing and stepping back will help you learn to enjoy the small pleasures in life. Spend some time with nature. One of my favourite poems is *Daffodils* by William Wordsworth. It goes like this...

"I wandered lonely as a cloud

That floats on high o'er vales and hills,

When all at once I saw a crowd,

A host, of golden daffodils."

This poem helps me pause and recreate the poet's vision of the daffodils in this peaceful place. Nature gives out a positive energy. You need to be open to receive it. Take time to visit a park or garden. Enjoy the colors, the texture of the grass, the flowers, the plants and trees around you. Feel their energy. Spending time with little children also gives you so much learning. They are pure and carefree in their disposition. They have no fear and learn to talk, and walk with curiosity, never afraid of failure or how others around them will judge them.

These techniques will help you remain in happiness and light irrespective of your surroundings. They help you stay in control.

Questions to ask about time management:

What if you decide not to procrastinate, but you have too many things in your plate?

Sometimes in life it is important to learn to say no, to accept that you are not the supermom or the superwoman or the superman. It is all right to be just human.

What if you want to get organized, but do not know where to start?

There are a lot of schedulers and organizers that can help you available either online or as printable tools. You have to invest the initial few hours of your time and then things start going like clockwork. It is also okay to ask for help. Get a friend who is good at organizing to give you some tips and start planning with you.

What if you are addicted to watching TV serials and it eats into your time?

This is a tricky one, because I have been there. There is no gain without pain. Discipline and reward systems work well. Tell yourself if you finish X amount of work, you will treat yourself to so many hours of TV time. The brain loves and craves for rewards and this becomes a win-win situation.

Action Steps

- *Assign 30 minutes every week as time well spent to plan the week, allotting extra time for random, urgent work that lands unexpectedly.*

- *Work in partnership with your spouse or your children or your friend, and plan the four boxes that define your work as important and urgent, important but not urgent, not important but urgent and not important, not urgent. Make it a fun craft activity with colored paper or pencils, fun stickers and so on. You will be surprised at the inputs you receive, which can make you redefine what you think is important and useful and what is not.*

- *Make sure to add "me time" in your list. Make time to pamper yourself in doing things that you enjoy, such as a spa date, a passion for sports or the arts. Fine tune your skills in these passions. This will give you that sense of satisfaction and happiness and fulfillment. This helps to serve you and serve others around you better and in happiness rather than in resentment.*

Notes

_____

_____

_____

_____

_____

_____

_____

_____

_____

_____

_____

_____

_____

_____

_____

_____

_____

SIX

Emotional Savvy

YOUR INTERNAL WORLD IS
FULL OF STORIES YOU PAINT

The power of perception

Your internal world is full of stories. The stories you tell yourself are based on your perceptions and built from your emotions and experiences. They have a deep effect on your stress, your performance, how you think, how you feel and how you behave.

Emotional agility is your ability to glide in and out of the maze of emotions, both positive and negative, accepting difficult ones with equal ease. Facing life without fear, with compassion and being curious and accepting.

People who have higher emotional agility find it easy to change and lead a happier and a successful life.

Emotions are often misunderstood and suppressed. As a young boy, if you fall down, in many cultures the little boy is told, "Don't cry, boys don't cry." In school you study mathematics, you study science and art, but there are no classes for learning about emotions.

You have been taught to suppress your hurt, your fear and your shame as a bad sign of weakness. As you grow, you block these strong emotions, especially the negative ones. All emotions are a natural part of you and whether comfortable or unpleasant, they're not to be suppressed.

It is okay to feel all the emotions. Articulating them provides a release. For example, it's okay to feel sad and cry at the loss of a loved one. Much research has been conducted on the physical and mental benefits of crying. It's okay to scream with joy when you pass an exam with flying colors. Emotional wellness is a state of being when you are attentive to your own thoughts and feelings, both the positive and the negative.

People need help to cope with stress in life, stress at work, stress in a relationship leading to poor physical and mental health. It influences how you think, act and feel. Emotional wellness promotes resilience, the ability to adapt to what life is offering you, the ability to trust and also to learn to set your own boundaries, the ability to say no and to learn new things, to love.

Understanding different emotions

Understanding emotions increases your self-esteem and confidence, leading to better relationships, better health and a greater and higher rate of success in all that you do. Emotional wellness is the quality of a leader. Happiness has been a much talked about emotion. It is independent of wealth. On a survey conducted in a workplace, being happy comes first on a list of people's reasons to stay in the job, despite a lower monetary gain.

Poor emotional health shows up as low self-esteem, low self-worth, being insecure, negative, moody and anxious. It promotes fear, the fear to fail, the fear to act, which both keep you from trying new things and living your life in resentment.

We often judge people superficially and decide whether we want to trust them or not. Many people start with mistrust. This may save them from being deceived. Fear is the biggest factor. Fear of what might happen. Fear of the unknown. Trust triggers the feel-good factor in the brain, which relaxes you. While caution is a useful habit, many times following instincts and trusting opens up opportunities.

All of us want to feel secure. Insecurity breeds anxiety. You feel insecure when you feel threatened, whether it's real or imaginary. Especially in a relationship, there can be difficult feelings such as jealousy. Building your self-esteem helps you keep a sense of security and self-respect and boosts your confidence. Start by trusting your capabilities. One fears the unknown. Being stuck in your perception does not allow you to open up. Deficiencies cause fear; such as a deficiency of love in a relationship, or a deficiency of money or confidence.

Being confident in your capabilities and taking life as it comes while staying positive helps you tide over your fear. Not being afraid to fail helps you learn. You begin to see opportunities in different places, which you may not have thought of before. Confidence expands your mind.

Observing your emotions and articulating them keeps you in touch with your feelings. It gives you the ability to think, process information and feel, all at the same time. It connects you with your feelings. This is what one calls emotional agility. Example: if you are happy, you will smile a lot and take positive actions. If you experience the emotion of anger you may shout and make a bad decision. It is okay to be angry, but what you do with the anger is more important. You can tell yourself or the other person that you are angry, what made you angry and you can express it in a nice way to them. This gives the other person the openness to receive it and allows them to see your point of view and offer their point of view in return. This helps in building relationships.

Soon there is a space for a conversation instead of a shouting match. It is a good way to be in touch with your emotions. Positive emotions positively affect your body. Homeostasis is a condition when the body is able to maintain balance for optimum functioning. The body reacts to the internal and external environment. The mind has a deep connect with the body. Any emotion creates a reaction in the body along with the mind. For example, joy relaxes the muscles in your body and is not seen as a threat by the brain. It helps the body maintain homeostasis. Fear on the other hand raises the heart rate in your body, making you anxious. The body recognizes it as a threat and all the energy in the body gets focussed on fighting it, instead of solving the actual problem at hand. It comes at a cost. It costs the cognitive, digestive and immune system to reduce function or to even shut down.

Although it is a natural and useful reaction at times, many people are constantly in fear. The mind gets trained to go into survival mode even with the slightest of triggers. Let us take Sonia's example, who we introduced in the first chapter. She is possessed by her smart phone, to the point where I wonder who is smarter, Sonia or her phone? She is stressed if she does not get likes for her Instagram post. She is constantly texting and browsing with her phone. Imagining that her battery will drain causes her to mentally panic. Her body is constantly stressed and in survival mode. This has a great impact on creating lifestyle diseases such as high blood pressure, type 2 diabetes and food intolerances. Most of these diseases are reversible. Practicing body and mind techniques such as yoga and meditation helps in keeping you healthy and focussed and your body and mind attuned to succeed instead of stress.

Dealing with stress using the imagination

When I am stressed it helps me to take a five minute timeout, a break, to close my eyes, observing my breath, which at that time is in a super-fast pace. I just observe. In my mind, I start imagining a favorite place of mine which gives me peace. For me it is an imaginary banyan tree, big and old with its branches spread wide and with aerial prop roots. It is beside a fish pond filled with a brilliant mix of orange, yellow, white, black and red koi. The birds perched on the trees are singing and I go and mentally sit under that tree and breathe and relax for a few minutes.

While all this imagination is happening in my mind, I physically start relaxing. Using this same image every time I'm stressed helps me ground myself and gives my mind the ability to get that balance and gives me the time to cope with the stress.

How the brain processes emotions

The average human brain has a hundred billion nerve cells, and a hundred trillion individual processes happen inside your body every second of your life. Each of these nerve cells seem to be capable of making around a thousand connections, which largely do the work of data storage. Multiply each of these hundred billion nerve cells by an approximate thousand connections they can make, and you can imagine the capacity of your brain.

Your brain increases in size until the age of 18 years and the only area that continues to grow after that is the hippocampus, supporting memory and encoding storage. One cannot say that memory fades with age. The process is more complex. The tendency to retain and recall emotional memories is stronger.

"Our emotions have a mind of their own, one which can hold views quite independently of our rational mind", says Daniel Goleman.

Most often, you learn to hide your emotions so well that even you don't recognize them. You may be sad and deeply hurt and overwhelmed, but it comes out as anger.

You may have noticed there are some people who try to be funny and loud in a party. They may not be the happy people as they would like to portray themselves. They could be actually lonely and they're couching that feeling and even unconscious of it. There's a tendency of denial and withdrawal when there is deep emotional hurt. The more you deny it, the more it comes to haunt you in different ways, like the feeling of being unworthy, not understood or not loved. As a result of this you can become aggressive and show temper tantrums or randomly exhibit irrational behavior which can be beyond their comprehension.

"Our feelings are not there to be cast out or conquered. They are there to be engaged and expressed with imagination and intelligence", are the wise words of T. K. Coleman.

Forgiveness is the first step to building trust

Learn to forgive. It is an important part of building trust. Learn to trust yourself and your intuitions. They give you valuable lessons. Learn to be happy. It comes from focussing in the present. The past has happened, learn to let go of it. Let go of the emotional baggage that does not help you especially if you have tried to fix it and given it your best shot and it is still not working. Adopt acceptance and stop being judgmental. Set your goals and focus on the present and give it your best. Be open about the future as there is no use worrying about something that no one can predict accurately. Learn to face your fear. Accept fear and anxiety. They serve their purpose in helping you define your limits and serve as your inbuilt survival mechanism. Begin to trust and be open to the unknown. This is where your fears will grip you most. Being adaptable and curious helps. Learn to expand your boundaries within reasonable limits and take baby steps in exploring.

Practice stress release techniques. Anything from a good massage, a good workout to practicing mindfulness.

The difference between empathy and agreeing with the other person

Empathy is the ability to see something from another person's point of view or another perspective. The part where people get confused is when you think you also have to agree to the other point of view. It is great to look at things from another perspective, to be able to feel what the other person feels and yet be able to disagree with that view.

You see a pin prick someone's finger and you feel the pain and distress. A nurse learns to block this feeling of distress to make herself fully present in the children's section or the ICU of the hospital. Too much empathy can lead to hurt. Imagine the life of the nurse if she started taking the pain of the patients in the hospital personally. This would put an undue amount of emotional stress on that nurse.

An appropriate amount of empathy is a good habit to acquire. You need to empathize with the other's emotions in a rational way.

For example, in an office setting, what would happen if one of your team members makes a colossal mistake? As a manager, you will get frustrated. You can be angry at the employee and take action. You can hope this will help the other team members learn and perform better. Expressing frustration may also relieve you of the anger and stress.

You think the employee has learnt the lesson. Ironically, this is not the case. Responding in anger and frustration erodes loyalty, makes all the other employees anxious and fearful, which signals to their brains to react as if they are under threat, which in turn inhibits cognitive thinking and inhibits creativity. Basically, their cognitive brain will shut down and the end result will be a dull non-productive team and an unhappy you.

Research has shown, however, that if you are able to be non-judgmental, and choose compassion, empathy and curiosity, it increases trust not only from the employee, but from the entire team. If the manager takes a moment before acting, this helps them contain the frustration regarding how as the manager they will be held responsible for the loss due to the employee's mistake. Instead, having a conversation with the employee to look into what happened, how can you now fix this situation and what they can do to ensure it does not happen again is a game changer. Doing this shifts the energy from blame and resentment to taking responsibility.

Focus on the moment by literally taking a deep slow breath or two, using your nostrils, which gives your brain the time to ground itself and to contain your anger and be able to put yourself in the employee's shoes. This way of thinking and taking action brings about trust and creative solutions from the employee and the team.

Empathy helps you to forgive, prevents your blood pressure from rising, increases team loyalty and a collaborative spirit, promotes creative thinking from both you and your team. It is a strong leadership building tool, making it a win-win situation for you.

Practical advice on how to show empathy to those around you

How do you show empathy? If you are home, ask your family members what you can do for them today. It shows that you care. The same applies if you are outside your home or at the office. Maybe, you think they need x or y or z. Maybe you think you know better, with your experience. However when you ask what they want, you are automatically enrolling and empowering them. You can now have a conversation about it. Maybe they will finally tell you what you had in mind. But you will earn their respect. Maybe through this process you realize that you were missing some points because of certain assumptions you had. This can be a good opportunity to expand your thoughts, your mind and for your personal growth. It is a pathway to happiness and stress free living.

Forgiveness and empathy does more good for you than it does for others. The forgiveness must be genuine and come from your heart. Forgiving in words but harboring the hurt, sadness and anger internalizes the feelings. In this case you are not sincere. This is not a healthy way to deal with hurt and is only a temporary solution to buying peace. You need to let go, more for your own good than for the other person. Forgiveness is not only about learning to forgive others, it is also about forgiving yourself. No one is perfect, and it is fine if you make mistakes. Don't get pulled into the blame game. You can learn from your mistakes, forgive yourself and start living in a positive frame of mind. This will make you see opportunities and give you the feeling of lightness in life.

Questions about your emotions:

What if you cannot control your anger even if you want to?

Anger is an emotion like many others. It is fine to be angry and accept that you are. It helps if you express your anger by telling yourself that you are angry. This gives it a vent. Sometimes the other person does not even know that you are angry. If you internalize it, people see that you are upset but do not understand what you are angry about. Telling the other person that you are angry and why lends clarity and definition and an opportunity to do something positive about it.

What if you are overwhelmed by stress? How can you then be happy?

Laughter is an antidote to stress. Some stress is good, it helps keep your deadlines and performance. Stress that kills your enthusiasm and makes you tired and depressed is bad stress.

You do not need a reason to laugh or even smile. You can fake it till you make it. Being happy releases happy hormones in your system that kills stress. Practice a big smiley face creates the feel of happiness in your body.

What if letting go of something hurtful is not easy. What can you do?

Imagine you walking around in the office, walking around at home, walking in the park and all the time carrying a big sack full of boulders. How does that feel? Does that help you? That is exactly what you are doing when you are not letting go. You are carrying a sack full of hurt. Hurt has happened in the past. Learn from it. Things do not always work as per your plan. Stop playing a victim and the blame game. Focussing on the present and what you can actively do today that is engaging and useful to you. If someone has hurt you and you try to let them know, but get no remorse or sorry from them, make peace with it. Know that you can still love them. That is a powerful feeling. Acceptance brings about lightness in your life and your ability to let go.

Action Steps

▶▶ *Join a laughter club or practice a smiley face and greet everyone with a big smile. It is the perception of happiness that fools your mind into thinking that you're happy.*

▶▶ *Challenge yourself to physical activities that help you face your fear. Your body and mind are one and it increases your mental ability to open up and be curious. Go try out skydiving, scuba diving or something else that you thought you never could do.*

▶▶ *When you are angry, go to the bathroom and scream at the mirror or kick the dustbin. It is a good outlet to release your anger. Once you have given vent to the initial anger, talk about why you were angry with this person or with yourself. If you get angry over silly reasons, you can even try being angry with a smiley face and that would be most hilarious. Try it out!*

Notes

_____

_____

_____

_____

_____

_____

_____

_____

_____

_____

_____

_____

_____

_____

_____

_____

_____

_____

SEVEN

Heart Meets Head

YOU ARE A FEELING BEING WITH AN ABILITY TO THINK

$$E = MC2$$

The balancing act

Finding a good balance between what you think and how you feel about it helps you understand yourself and the people around you.

Too much attention to thoughts makes you disconnected with reality and too many emotions make you focus on others and make you lose yourself in the bargain. This is according to a study on emotions by psychologists Myriam Bechtoldt and Vanessa Schneider. People think with their head and feel with their heart. Thinking comes from your logical and cognitive abilities. Over the past few hundred years, humanity has been training its brains to be logical and with scientifically- oriented thinking and not to believe in anything without valid proof.

One plus one is always two, not three. If it is three it needs to be substantiated by proof. There are no miracles or magic in life. This has led to wonderful discoveries and inventions making today's world a much more comfortable place to live in. From street lights to computers to artificial intelligence, like drones and driverless vehicles. In this bargain, however, you may have neglected the feeling part of your brain. Emotions help you feel, connect to and perceive the world around you. Feeling does not necessarily follow logic and proof. Sometimes magic happens and because there is no logic does not mean it is not true. Thinking and feeling together completes you as a person.

The head is for reasoning, intelligence and knowledge, and the heart is for feeling, empathy and compassion: these two aspects form your personality. Using the head alone is not enough to succeed. A combination of a head and a heart helps you understand the world in its entirety. It helps you think and also adds the dimensions of feeling, trust and intuition that help you navigate in the future.

I learn how to stay in the moment from my canine friend, Casper. Casper is our small sized Maltese terrier and this year he turns 17. His vision is partially impaired in one eye and completely gone from the other. His olfactory abilities are close to nil. Yet he walks around the house like he's the king. I see him trotting into the wall, hitting his head and walking in the other direction as if nothing happened. He goes around and round the garden in circles, unable to orient himself towards the door to come inside the house. Yet, I do not see him frustrated or angry. He finally gets to where he wants to go. He goes to his small dog house and rests. Only to repeat the entire routine again after a few hours.

Casper when young was a typical alpha dog, taking upon himself to protect his master, my daughter. I see him just as zesty in life as he was when he came home some 17 years ago. He reminds me every day how one can remain in the present, irrespective of the circumstances surrounding.

The cognitive part of your brain is for processing and solving problems

The cognitive and logical ability of your mind helps in processing the world around you and helps you analyze and solve problems. It helps you make quick decisions. You are more focussed, task oriented and productive. It makes you decide objectively and get to the point. Over the past 100 years humanity has been focussing and developing this skill and it has helped science discover and invent various theories and devices to improve the quality of life.

You can now order food online and it arrives at your home. Two generations ago you had to grow your own vegetables and fruits and livestock and milk your own cows. Maybe you had to go to the local market to pick up the produce and then cook your daily meal. Is your life better now than during your grandma's time? Is your life stress free now? Did money and conveniences buy you happiness?

The emotional part of the brain has been neglected

Emotions and feelings are also a part of you. It is, however, the part that has not been given an equal amount of importance as the thinking part. Feeling helps you connect to the social world and helps you show empathy and compassion. It helps you define a value to life. You can make equally good decisions based on intuitions. The decisions are value based and from the heart. In spite of all the facilities and conveniences in this life, life is full of stress.

Emotions like trust, empathy, joy, anger, frustration and compassion are all valid and to be acknowledged and handled. They teach you the perseverance and grit needed to be achievers.

Often a combination of thinking and feeling is what makes one more complete. You have to learn to be in touch with your emotions as it is a skill you have not acquired or has not been taught to you when you were young.

In order to demonstrate how this works, let us use the example of two salesmen. The first salesman explains how perfect and unique his product is and the second starts a sales pitch enquiring about your needs and even chats with you about the weather. The second salesman is more likely to sell the product, even if what he is offering is not as great as the first one.

What is being in the moment? Your past teaches you lessons, some sweet and some not so sweet. You often live in those past moments, reliving them again and again in resentment. Using the lessons learnt to move on is not easy. However, learning how to move on and to be open, makes you see the opportunities in everything around you. It is good to have a goal and a future plan, but no one can predict the future. Use your head to think, analyze and plan. However, this in itself is not enough. You also need to use your heart to use compassion, empathy and trust and be positive. Emotion helps build your self-esteem and confidence needed to succeed in your plan and give you the grit and determination to be open and adapt and to go with the unknown future.

Using your head and heart together helps you become mindful of the present. You become a better observer and choose your actions. This decreases your stress and helps you in achieving happiness.

Emotions are demonstrated physically. If you feel an emotion, your body reacts by laughing or crying. If you breathe in a certain way, tears can start flowing from your eyes as if you were crying, even without your heart feeling sad in the first place, or without a reason to feel sad. If you use your facial muscles and engage your cheeks to keep an expression of a smile, you begin to feel happy. You can generate your happiness with your muscles without a reason.

Carl Sagan says, "Science is a way of thinking, much more than it is a body of knowledge".

Using your head and heart together

When you perceive threats, you start thinking and acting without cognition and deep consideration. Many times, these serve to handle the momentary situation, but as a long term solution, they often fall short.

Sometimes highly emotional decisions do not serve us. For example, you come home from work tired only to see your children playing the X-Box instead of studying for an exam. You're furious and yell at them. Maybe your kid will study in fear at that moment, but did you check why the child was playing? Did he or she finish their studies? If not, did you set the boundaries and the repercussions for the child, and do you follow through with it? What will the child learn from your behavior? You cannot teach children; they learn by observing you. Give a moment to yourself instead of immediately reacting.

Use your heart and head to understand. Think and feel what is happening and what is the best action. Once you feel you are in control and can choose your action, if shouting is the best action then go ahead by all means. That moment of time, which helps brings your heart and head together, allows you to be in control and make the right choice.

What is the difference between knowledge and wisdom? "Knowledge is gained by gathering data, whereas wisdom is earned by going through actual life experience", says Master Jin Kwon.

How do you use your head and heart to work together? Look at anger, for instance. Look out for triggers. As stated in an earlier chapter, in an office atmosphere for example when a conversation is not going your way, excuse yourself for a minute. Get up, dust your suit off and sit down again. It's as simple as that. If you can go for a walk in the office hallway or the garden, if there is one nearby, do that and come back after you've recollected your thoughts.

This simple action gives you the precious few seconds to be in control. Not to mention that it also gives others a few moments to think and recollect their own thoughts as well. It's a win-win situation. It's okay to get angry and then acknowledge it, because there may be a valid reason. Once you get the few seconds you need, your immediate reaction to shout or react irrationally is gone. Now you can articulate your reason for disagreeing with your colleague and be open to their point of view. If they disagree with your point, be gracious and say, "thank you" to them for sharing their view. Try and analyze their reasoning. This energy you create helps a bad atmosphere pass as you are using your heart and head.

If you are the type who likes to follow rules and get stuck over analyzing, you will notice that this habit causes a lot of stress and is non-productive.

Managing rules with both your heart and your head

There are rules and it is very important to follow them. If you are the personnel manager in a big firm, for example, it is natural for you to ensure that the leave routine is followed as per the book. If someone applies for a few days of leave over what is available to them, don't turn them down just because the rule book says so. Instead of simply turning their request down without an explanation, you can show some caring and check for a reason before you take any action or make a decision. Even if you have to decline the leave request at the end of it all, the other person will not be that offended, and they will be touched by your sincerity.

The left side of your brain is logic driven and the right side of the brain is the creative side. Collectively you function as one whole, your body and mind, or your heart and head together. Your body is a useful tool to help you connect to your mind. You are trained from a young age to focus on the thinking and the logical part of the brain and thus it is more developed. This left part of the brain is focussed on methodical, analytical thinking, mathematics, thinking in words and facts.

The right side of your brain is connected with creativity, intuition, visualization and rhythm. Your limbic system focusses on emotions and memories. Developing the limbic system trains your logical and thinking part of the brain to coexist with the creative part. More than 70% of people use this creative side of the brain poorly and only live in the thinking world.

Keeping different parts of your brain active with mental stimulation is necessary to generate new brain cells. Learning new skills like picking up a new language, learning to play the piano, playing memory games, taking up new hobbies like gardening, golf or even playing video games activate different parts of the brains, especially those areas that are not normally used. Learning to relax, keep "me time" and do nothing or do some fun things like meeting your friends for a Karaoke singing is also very helpful for getting the head and heart to work together.

Somatics, or movement therapy, is learning to use and interact with your body in a way that helps you connect it with your mind. Language is generative, it always creates responses and therefore more language. When you say certain things, you will get certain responses. If I were to tell you that your dress sense is terrible, you are going to get defensive, annoyed and angry. My use of words has generated a reaction, in this case, a negative emotion in you. Instead, if I were to ask you if you would like to try out a different style and combination of clothes, you might at least acknowledge my suggestion with a "thank you" and perhaps give it a thought.

There are different types of somatic exercises you can try. If you change your facial muscles to show a smile, even if you are not happy you start to feel happy. You don't need a reason to actually feel happy. This means you can use your body to make you experience happiness. In fact, breathing in a particular pattern, exhaling quickly in a set of three, with your mouth open, it seems like you are laughing and fools your body to be happy. Similarly, a set of three short inhalations can soon bring tears in your eyes and you begin to feel sad, again without a valid reason.

Dance, for example, is another somatic exercise. Not only does it provide a good body workout, it does wonders for your mind. It can take you to a trance. The University of London found a positive impact of dance on anxious and stressed people. Dance is a way people can release their stress when with an open attitude by enjoying every moment of it. Sometimes watching a ballet moves people to tears. They also found people who practiced dancing recovered faster from heart surgery. Dance has a cathartic effect on people.

Music is used in vibrational therapy for healing. It can be seen in the chanting practices of Mayans, Egyptians, Indian, Chinese and Japanese cultures. It's also seen in the shamanistic practices of Native American Indians, the people of Tibet and Australian Aborigines. These groups have been known to use sound therapy for healing. Emotional stress has a negative effect on our subtle energy. Noise pollution from traffic, construction sites, sirens, and even from mobile phones causes energy imbalance. Some types of music, vocal and instrumental, have a profound calming effect. The classical compositions of Bach and Beethoven, use strictly defined patterns that resonate with your ears and brains, and the music produces a calming effect in your body. Music consisting of alpha and theta waves help the meditative and creative part of the brain. The use of tones, the vibratory notes from vowels and use of "mmm" endings, are found in the Vedic Indian system used in the Aum chanting and is also incorporated in the Muslim prayer call. The use of overtones is found in Tibetan chants and some Gregorian hymns.

Yoga is a complete mind-body workout. By holding yoga positions for a few counts, you learn stability, balance, strengthening and agility of the body. Yoga increases mental concentration abilities. A set of two poses always involves a combination of two opposites like inhaling and exhaling, contracting and expanding of muscles. Each pose requires you to focus in the moment.

These tools and techniques help your head and heart meet in a central point, allowing you to be in sync with your creative and cognitive side, helping you to make balanced and focussed decisions in clarity and lightness.

Questions to help you align your head and your heart:

What if you cannot stop thinking about your family's future and financial stability and you become anxious all the time?

It is a good idea to invest some time to set your future goals and plan your finances with a budget that includes setting aside a percentage for surprises. Make it a practice and don't be overly ambitious with your budget. Don't over think and over analyze it, if creating a budget makes you feel anxious.

Since no one can be sure of what their future holds, worrying unnecessarily about the future is not helpful. Instead, feeling positive promotes an attitude of confidence that shows in the way you are, how you think, and how you act. Being positive helps your brain make clever choices that slowly help you build a better future on a foundation of lightness instead of anxiety.

What if you believe that people will think you are a non-performer if you are not seen as being busy and stressed in the office?

Most people, including successful people, are filled with stress. Stress seems to be synonymous with success. Almost like a package deal. It is natural to perceive calm people as non-performers. But with calmness also comes confidence and increase in self-esteem and to take well thought of and value-based judgement that boosts performance.

What if you are focussed and analytical and create the best solution and product, yet you do not win any sales contracts?

According to your assessment, analysis and studies, your product is the best, however, have you checked what the buyer needs? Have you tried connecting with them, chatting with them and finding details on what their needs are? Have you also included a personal touch by asking about their health or discussing about the weekend game perhaps?

This is how you connect to people with your heart and use your head to then analyze and formulate and offer a product.

Win their trust. It might take a couple of sales calls, before you are awarded the project, but you stand a better chance than if you directly say, "Hello, I have this product and it is best because it takes care of your needs" and so on, without even checking notes with the buyer's actual needs.

Actin Steps

▶▶ *Be curious. It helps you learn and understand from another point of view. Ask a lot of "what" questions rather than "why" questions. "Why" questions trigger the defence mechanism in people and they will shut you down. Whereas "what" questions make them think and give you better answers. "Why" makes them defensive. When people speak, learn to listen instead of judging them and giving your opinion before they even complete a sentence.*

▶▶ *Forgiveness prompts you to let go of the pain and hurt from the past. Learn your lessons and move on. It makes you a happier and lighter person. Move on from the thought of what you want and the way you want the other person to be or behave, or the way you want somethings to be. Apologize if you have knowingly or unknowingly hurt someone. It helps the other person let go of their anger and gives a chance to clear up the misunderstanding and build the bridge.*

▶▶ *Learn from your mistakes and focus on what you can change and what is in your power to change. Just keep a positive attitude.*

Notes

EIGHT

Effortless Relationships

RELATIONSHIP IS A TANGO. IT TAKES TWO TO MAKE A DANCE

What is a relationship?

A relationship is like a dance where the two people have to be coordinated in their thoughts and actions. They have to learn to synchronize each step with the other, be supportive and move effortlessly and gracefully as if they are one.

A relationship is when two people connect and correlate. They see and feel some connection, in spite of not looking or thinking the same or even belonging to the same background. This connection helps them to share their thoughts effortlessly and together they nourish each other to become better and more mature human beings in joy and peace. In a relationship based on love, there is no one better or bigger than the other.

It works on the principle of equals. If two people become one, two different people become one. The effort may not be equal at all times, but this is not a competition. It has to be looked at like a dance. There's no pressure between the partners as they dance. The pull and push is accomplished with grace.

The ego dissolves when two become one. That is what makes relationships effortless. This is easier to read than achieve. Nothing good in life comes easy. It is about the willingness to let go of your ego, be inquisitive and willing to learn new ways without getting the ego in the way and still standing strong and as an individual, happy and confident.

My background and my relationship

It took me years to get where I am today. I met my husband Ramesh when I was 21 years old. Maybe it was love at first sight. Maybe it was youth and naivety or maybe I just wanted to experiment. One will never know, but whatever the reason, I said yes.

My husband is what I am not. Okay, maybe opposites attract? What is the impact of such an attraction. Nobody prepared me for that. Concepts like empathy and compromise were alien to the younger me. Many times, we agreed on things, but during the times we did not agree, I felt because I was right, he was wrong, naturally.

Most of the time I would give up because I didn't care less, or I would go to the other extreme and fight tooth and nail until he gave up. Either way sometimes it led to deep resentment and lack of joy in the relationship. Much later I realized "I" was the reason. My ego. I didn't want to give up who I am. I didn't want to change, because I was always right. Ramesh was always more understanding, supporting and the giving one in the relationship.

Life went on through the ups and downs and some frustrating moments, until my "aha" moment came. When my mentor asked me, "What makes you think you're always right when you give that wonderful advice to your family and what makes you think you can fix it all?"

I was silent for the longest time. I worked from there, learning what it means to let go of your ego and understand that everybody is equal and has an equal opportunity in voicing their opinion of value. My life changed and continues to change for the better till today. I learned the art of submission and to let go. It's not because I'm weak, but because I'm strong and confident as I define the broad framework of what I want and how much I'm willing to be flexible in life. It's my choice. I welcome the unknown with an open mind, peacefully accepting what I do not know. Saying I'm okay with it as there are some things one can never comprehend. And it's okay.

This gives me a positive outlook and the emotional agility to dance in a relationship with joy. A relationship is a place where you share to grow. A husband-wife relationship is more personal than a business relationship but there is a lot to learn in both relationships.

Why it's important to be different to your partner

People say, opposites attract. Imagine you are married to a person who agrees with everything you say and do. Where is the spice in life? Where is the growth? In a relationship you try and see the world from another perspective. You learn a lot more about yourself, no right or wrong, just different. Then you learn to share your views. This openness helps expand your mind. Being open helps build a beautiful bond for life, with sharing and caring.

Humans are social beings. A good relationship helps you get physical and mental security and is important for your wellbeing. A relationship is like two-way traffic. When there is love, there can be 99% give and 1% take at times and the opposite at other times. You need to be able to dance with your partner and find the right balance. A good relationship forms a good support system physically, mentally and financially too.

A good relationship has a positive impact on your health. The mental stability and comfort it provides you helps your body to relax and enjoy the moment. Relationships let you experience something new. When two people are involved you experience things that you are not used to and learn something new in the journey of life. A strong relationship is where your individuality is nourished, in spite of giving to the relationship.

Relationships give you maturity and help you age gracefully. A study from the University of Missouri found that people were happier, matured and grew older gracefully with a partner, rather than if they had been alone or in an unhappy relationship. Being emotionally and physically healthy reduces your chances of heart attacks. It also helps you have a better quality of sleep.

Even in a good relationship, 70% of the relationship problems never get solved. Most relationship issues are the kind that need to be worked around, rather than being solved.

"Never allow someone to be your priority while allowing yourself to be their option", said Mark Twain.

Why relationships fail

The most common reason for a relationship to fail is trust issues. Jealousy, rigidity, different expectations, different priorities, different pace, communication issues, narcissism, physical and mental abuse, boredom and a lack of love and financial and health related issues. It may not be easy to share. You cannot share your bed, your thoughts and your feelings, unless you establish trust in the relationship.

Trust also translates to accepting the other as he or she is, and sharing makes the bond stronger where both can change together. If you do not give your 100% in a relationship, it will show. Cracks develop in a relationship that has insincerity. There is no growth in such a relationship and the love you initially felt soon disappears.

It leads to boredom, infidelity and unhappiness. This affects your health and your performance at work. You start looking for quick fix solutions, which strangely do not include communicating with the other person. People either move away from such strained relationships or stay in them in misery. It becomes the same old routine when there are two people in a room but there's no energy there.

Where there is no understanding, empathy or maturity, internal growth stops. There's no enthusiasm, there is only negative energy left in the relationship.

"The meeting of two personalities is like the contact of two chemical substances. If there is any reaction, both are transformed." This quote from Carl Jung brings out the deep bond a relationship can make. Ego is a big culprit that comes between relationships. When one partner wants to prove they are better than the other, or when one partner gets a promotion and the other is jealous instead of being happy, or sometimes it becomes the question of who will give up or say sorry first in a fight.

The ego must dissolve in a relationship based on love

In a relationship of love, there can be no ego. They are two souls being one. It is okay to lose, or say sorry, or not be in the same level as someone you love. Let go of your ego. Try and understand what the other person wants. Showing compassion helps build a relationship. Creating family values works in strengthening the relationship. The value of trust, loyalty, mutual respect, appreciation and integrity.

Family values add contentment to your framework of how you think and act as a team. It holds the relationship together and inspires both of you to be better partners.

Sharing is caring. Discussing your goals and arriving at solutions to some common pain points help increase understanding and reduces friction. This is better than leaving these things to one's imagination and assumptions. You can discuss and divide the household chores and arrive at a plan using a chart, which shows items such as who will drop the children off at school and on which days, sharing of programs on TV or the internet. Discussing key issues of conflict, however small they may seem to be.

Twice a week her TV shows, twice a week his TV shows and the other times it can be mutually decided at the moment. With the arrival of gadgets like iPads, it allows the individual to watch shows of their choice simultaneously sitting in the same room. This does rob one of the funs of give and take and sharing. Sharing helps in adding to the connection between the two individuals. Making life more fun while allowing you to learn to be flexible.

Flexibility teaches you to be adaptable and change with time. The other advantages of sharing the household chores like dusting, ironing, especially when you assign a special time during the week or in the weekends, it becomes a relaxing type of Zen meditation.

Emotional abuse in relationships

What is emotional abuse? How do you react to emotional abuse? Do you suppress a deep negative wound and unconsciously allow it to fester with you? Is it something you cannot deal with and neither get rid of? Do you often unload your emotional garbage to the people around you? Do you put a brave image and bury these feelings at the bottom of your heart? Or do you also partake in emotional abuse but directed to the weakest link you can find, more as a source of revenge? If you were the victim, you can make someone else the victim too, and you might feel momentary satisfaction.

Imagine a situation where your boss is firing you for the bad performance of your team, or maybe because he is having a bad day. This happens too often for your liking. You constantly go to the office in frustration and resentment. You are unable to be fully productive in the office. Do you come home in the same negative mood and you react to your spouse and children with that grumpy attitude. Does that resonate with you?

Repeated verbal attacks, humiliation, blame, being treated in a way that diminishes your dignity and self-worth comes under the definition of emotional abuse. People who are emotionally abusing others may not even be aware of this pattern. Emotional abuse can also cause more and deeper harm than physical abuse.

Do you get teased and bullied often and treated in a mean way? Are your views often ridiculed and disregarded? Is the other person often acidic and sarcastic? Do you get shamed and feel controlled by the other person, especially without your permission? Is the other person overbearing, not allowing you to express your views and if you do express them, they are ridiculed? Are your choices in life controlled, right down to what you wear, where and on what you spend your money and time, where you go, who your friends are? Is this happening despite that you are an adult? Do you feel like you are being treated as inferior?

Parents can shame their children by constantly comparing them with a sibling. They can inflict harsh punishments, sometimes even physical ones, on a child. These actions hurt deeply and remain with you throughout your life. The scars they leave can become fresh wounds later in life where you strongly react to such abuse by either being a bully or working against bullies. A child needs love. Children are here to learn from mistakes just like you did. They need constant reassurance of love, parents' support and encouragement. They do not need to be reprimanded all the time.

Emotional abuse, especially in an adult relationship, can lead to fear, anxiety, lack of sleep and depression. The more you give in, the more the other person will abuse you. Your self-esteem will be so low that you will lack the confidence to take the first step out. Many times people justify such behavior from their partner and are caught in the emotional net, unable to escape. Follow your instincts, and however hard it might be, accept reality and then take a corrective step as that is the only thing that helps. Seek professional help. If trying to improve the partner does not work, maybe you need to take some tough steps.

Emotional abusers are good manipulators. Look for the trap. Don't get into the blame game and blame yourself for the other's behavior. It is the other person who is weak and is trying to cover his or her weakness or fear by bulling and emotional manipulation. Your safety and wellbeing come first. Keep some emergency contact numbers handy. Learn to stand up for yourself. You have to respect yourself and know that you are worthy and capable. The other courses of action will follow.

Some people react to emotional abuse by ignoring the subject or burying it deep inside. Disconnecting is a good defence mechanism. It numbs your mind and gives it temporary relief from unpleasant situations and memories. Instead it comes out as resentment and bitterness. Some people deal with emotional abuse in a passive aggressive mode. This is not helpful in the long run, as it is then often a struggle as to who can push the most. The key to dealing with it is not by negativity. First seek help. Find a good therapist, surround yourself with good friends and supportive family members. Once you are in control of the situation, learning to forgive and let go is a major part of the healing process.

Questions to help you with your relationship:

What if you have done your MBA in finance, but your partner does not have any financial background? You cannot take your partner's advice when it comes to money matters.

Your partner may not have theoretical knowledge, but have you checked to see if your partner has any practical knowledge? Have you tried to share information with your partner? It is your ego that may think you know better than your partner. Ego judges, manipulates and leads you to quarrels, frustration, passive-aggression and mistrust.

Notice when your ego is at play. Observe, step back and take a deep breath. Show empathy, try and find out what the other person wants instead of sharing what you want and how you want to deal with the matter, because you think you know better.

What if you are both so busy in your lives, juggling finances, family, career and at the end of the day you just want quiet?

There will be days when "me time" is a good idea, but how about having a conversation with your partner about it. Learn to share information, sharing about your day, listening patiently to your partner without judgement and without interference, without being distracted by the smart phone while you are having a conversation. This gives them a sense of relaxation and relief from their daily struggle, even if there are no answers to their problem. Then you can request the same when you want to vent about your day.

If you want this deep listening from your partner, you have to live by the same rules too. This is how sharing is caring. If you want a patient ear from your partner, it is exactly what you will need to provide to your partner.

Setting up a romantic date with your partner once in a while gives you an escape from the monotony and stress of the real world. It helps give the time needed to build the relationship and keep it nourished.

Keeping your smart phone to charge in a far corner of the bedroom or in any room other than your bedroom helps in this day and age, when it has become a big source of distraction and robs one of precious time and can seriously get in the way of a relationship.

Your partner knows that you love him/her, why should you repeatedly tell him/her that you do?

Verbalising your emotions gives them validity. It connects the way you think to the way you feel. Saying "I love you" is a constant validation of love, which in a relationship, over the months and years tends to be easily taken for granted and missed.

Action Steps

▶▶ *Cuddling triggers the same amount of neurological reaction as pain killers. Use cuddles in your relationship, be it with your spouse or your children. You can give a warm hug to your friends when you meet them as well. It makes a big difference.*

▶▶ *It is a good practice to discuss with your partner how your day went before you retire at night. Try and talk about the fights and arguments before you sleep and don't keep them for another day. Try and be fair and be generous.*

▶▶ *Everyday find at least 10 ways to be grateful and show appreciation and love to your partner and family. Say out loud "I love you" to them. You can be grateful that your partner made the bed or tea today, or you can be grateful for the wonderful smile you received from your children when you came home tired from work. This feeling of gratitude will send a positive energy around you and will come back to you as a joyful relationship.*

Notes

NINE

Parenting Superstar

Are you a perfect parent?

The decision to be a parent entails huge responsibilities. It also comes with rewards. Planning and preparing for this responsibility helps to make it fun, an engaging and a delightful experience. It helps to invest in planning your time, resources and finances while sharing responsibility between both parents.

Nothing prepares you for turning your life upside down when the bundle of joy arrives. In order to nourish a complete family, you have to nourish yourself first, physically, mentally and emotionally. Letting go of your dreams for that of a child can only bring resentment in the parent. On the other hand, making objective decisions before becoming a parent helps you enjoy parenthood.

You can have your life and be a parent too. There is always a give and a take. In parenting the take is the child itself and it's all about the balance and getting it right. You learn a lot through your children.

My experiences as a parent

When Ritesh, our first child was born, we could not stop looking at the small wonder that we had brought to life. We were awe struck. He had a good mix of both our features. We brought him up like he was the first child in the universe, with so much love and care. We cherish that special first time experience of being a parent forever.

Along with special time came lack of sleep, moments of anxiety when he began to cry, and we did not know why. But his gurgling laughter made up for it all. As he grew, we as parents decided to give him the value of respect, trust, love and caring. We allowed him to learn through his mistakes, giving him a long rope with some boundaries, while educating him on societal norms. As he grew into a young adult and was older, stronger and wiser, he taught us what it means to respectfully let go. We had to learn to let go, and it initially came as a shock to us, despite being mentally prepared. Once children grow up to be young adults, you have to allow them to make their own choices and make their own mistakes. That is the biggest favor you can do for them.

You respect them, and they love and respect you even more. Allow them to make the mistakes and let them know you are always there for them, to protect them and be by their side.

Anisha is our second born child. She was a happy child. She still is. When she was young and had to write five lines on "My Mother", I can never forget a line from the essay. She wrote, "My mother eats and sleeps." I used to work part time and be home for the children when they were young. When they were back from school in the afternoon, I made sure they ate well and I encouraged them to nap, while I napped with them too. I burst out laughing at her observation skill, but it made me think in amazement, what children pick up from you.

You learn a lot from your children

Being a parent gives an opportunity for you to respect and appreciate your own parents. You may not agree with them, but that's okay. Being in that shoe helps you comprehend what it takes to be a parent. Children make you better human beings. I believe they are a gift from God and we don't own them. They're here to teach us. They bring out the loving, sharing and caring part of you. The more you give unconditional love the more love you receive.

They teach you the art of letting go as they grow older and stronger. They enrich you emotionally, giving you the ability to connect. Having children increases your self-esteem. This ability to let go and to connect are important life skills to have if you want to succeed in anything you do in life. Being a parent and having children makes you younger at heart. You're constantly interacting with the younger mind. The opportunities to go out and be physically active are equally enjoyable. Having children helps you be alert physically and mentally. You need to be one up on the information and open to change, to understand the younger generation and appreciate their outlook on life. Your life becomes exciting. You have to better manage your resources, like sleep and money and time.

There will also be family issues and challenges, but the reward of love makes up for it all. It humbles you to think that another life completely depends on you to nourish him or her. The joy of the smile and the warm cuddles from your children compare to nothing in this world. You develop the power to empathize. Quite frankly, there's never a dull moment as a parent.

There's no perfect family. There is no need to judge and be harsh on yourself. You make mistakes and you're constantly learning not only as parents but also as children. Be it family fights, politics, love, laughter and celebration. You can set the children free, but that emotional connect is the sweetest and will always remain.

You develop the power of being resilient. You can read as many child rearing and child psychology books as you want, but the fact is that your child has not read any of it and does not follow any of it either.

As Bill Ayers says, "Your kids require you most of all to love them for who they are. Not to spend your whole time trying to correct them".

Managing your energy as a parent

As a parent and especially a young parent, your energy has to be carefully managed. Your energy gets consumed by the children who are totally dependent on you at the time. You get limited time to pursue things that are important to you. You need a great amount of physical and mental energy and a lot of time management skills. Your goals need to be recalibrated to accommodate the children. A high degree of planning is required, otherwise your life can go upside down. Many vacations and outdoor activities are formed around what suits your children and what they like.

Plan your parenting well in advance. Reset your goals, taking into consideration the time you need to initially invest in bringing up a child. Prioritize and spend time planning your resources and finances. Share responsibility as parents. Deciding who does what in advance helps. For example, parent-teacher meetings can be attended by parents in an alternate rota system.

I totally believe in this quote from Wayne Dyer, "Your children are not your children. They come through you, but they are life waiting to express itself".

Your children come to this world through you, but that does not mean you own them. If you want respect, show respect. As they grow up, you cannot keep advising them, because sometimes advice sounds like a threat to them. It is like telling them that you know it all and they don't.

Teenagers are especially sensitive, wanting to rebel and be loved at the same time. As discussed earlier, language is generative, and it is the art of talking that is important and useful here.

Creating boundaries is a good tool for parenting. You can give your children or teenagers some degree of freedom, but make sure you clearly tell them the consequences of not following some rules and follow through on the consequences of breaking those rules. The consequences could be small yet significant things like taking away TV time privilege or outings with friends. It need not be something severe that scars the child. It need not be anything hurting or radical. If you're too strict, the children will tend to lie to escape the punishment or the shame of it.

Helping your child set goals and targets make them achievers. Show them that it is okay to fail and to learn from failure. Be a role model for them. At no age do you stop being a parent and there is no age that you stop learning to be a better parent. Each day, I still continue to learn new tricks in this role. I find that the more I enrich myself with personal growth, the more I think I can be available for my grown-up children, just by being there as a support whenever they need me.

The role of judgement in raising children

If somebody is not equal to you, in your perception, you tend to judge them. You feel either weaker or superior to others. When there is some form of neglect, or rejection of love, maybe early in your childhood, you end up feeling insecure. This leads to fear and you handle it by being defensive and aggressive or even by being a bully. Many times, parents unwittingly compare children. "Your sister is smarter than you. Your friend gets better grades than you, you are so stupid."So you start to feel inferior. You start getting disconnected with people.

Deep inside, each one of us seeks pure love and is also made of pure love. Look at little children to realize what innocence and pure love is. The less you judge, the more chances there are to feel this connect and this love.

Listening without judgement

Deep listening is about listening patiently without judgement. Are you judging the other person while he or she is talking? What is the conversation running in your mind? Are you paying your full attention to what the other person is trying to convey? How many times have you interrupted, not allowing the other person to complete their sentence?

Deep listening happens when you listen to what the other person has to convey, without interrupting them and without building stories in your mind while the other person is talking. Deep listening is letting the other completely convey what they want to convey. Then you can assess without judgement. Being curious helps. What is the other person trying to tell you? What subtle message is your child telling you with his pranks and out of the way behavior? Are you hearing it with your filters? What are your filters of hearing? What story about the other person or the situation is clouding your mind? What are your assessments about the situation or the person telling the story. Just by being curious about your thought process and being mindful and focussed in the present helps you be a better listener, a better person, a better parent.

When you are a better listener, you can hear the conversation from another perspective. That does not mean you agree with the other perspective. It makes you aware of another perspective. Listening in openness allows you to empathise. It allows you to be more flexible in your thought and action.

What are you thinking when you interrupt a conversation, or your children interrupt your conversation? Are you trying to control? Are you trying to impose your view on others, even if it is unconscious to you right now? Is it because you think you know better? This maybe because you have more experience, or it maybe because you have validated your thoughts with your experiences. But again, experiences are created by you with your assumptions and the stories you build in your mind. By telling your children, especially a teenager what they must do and what they must follow, you are unconsciously passing the message that you don't trust them, and this is not good for their self-esteem. If the teenager needs guidance, there are better ways than just pushing your method on them. You may think it is quicker to just raise your voice or use your position of authority as a parent and quickly get the work done the way you think works best for your children, but this is not always the case.

When you are not living in the present moment, your mind is already filled with some past story, often stressful, repeating again and again in a loop. Or you are living in the future, worrying about something not in your control. When you listen to a conversation with stress, you are not really listening. You are waiting for the other person to shut up. You are irritated and closed in your mind. You will get nothing of value from the conversation, and in short will be stuck where you are, there is no change and there is no creative outcome. This leads to more stress, mistrust, frustration and resentment.

My new mantra is, "I am not perfect". I consider every other human being as intelligent as I am and capable of finding a solution to a problem. Once I process a conversation with this thought, my listening skills start improving. I tend to be less judgmental. I start seeing things and appreciating it from another perspective. I try and co create good ways of being with my children. I earn the respect of my children.

It is a good idea to paraphrase what the other person was trying to express. Often, we assume and presume what the other person wants to convey, especially when it comes to your children. Paraphrasing ensures both of you are on the same page.

It is a good idea to pace a conversation instead of giving your advice at random. Pacing allows the other person to build trust in you when you do not interrupt their flow of thoughts and they will share more. If you have to give advice, you can ask for the other person's permission if they are adults. With children, you can open a conversation around it. Keep your boundaries clear so the children know their limits and where not to step out of line. This makes you an assertive parent as opposed to a controlling parent. You give a reflective mode to the conversation by clarifying what you heard and what you think while asking for their point of view. This will lend the dimension of respect and appreciative energy to the conversation and make it a more powerful one. This is something you can reflect on deeper and come to your own conclusions about.

Questions to help you with parenting:

What if you are not a good or capable parent?

No one is a perfect parent. There is no right or wrong way. You learn from your mistakes. What keeps the family together is love and respect and the power of sharing and caring. Trust your instincts.

What if your neighbor's child has done so well in his class, why can't your child be like hers?

Comparing children is the most demotivating factor for the child. What makes children succeed is the love, compassion and understanding shown by their parents and the acceptance, the desire to be accepted. They just want the "okay" nod from the parents. Keep looking at the smallest of achievements and tell them how amazing they are. This builds their self-confidence and motivates them to be better performers.

What if you have such a tight schedule and a hectic plan for your career. How can you make time for your children?

Planning right and some hard work can help you find the answers to be a career focussed parent. Outsource help. Many organizations have parents and especially new mom-friendly policies. Seek the support of your parents, friends, your community. Go off the guilt trip. There is no substitute for quantity time, but sometimes giving quality time to your children gives you the flexibility to follow your dreams and is more beneficial for the children in the long run.

Action Steps

▶▶ *Every evening, spend some time planning the next morning's routine and schedule for yourself and your children. This makes life less chaotic and much easier to manage. Invest in a family organizer. They come with all the color codes possible. Mark your meetings, your children's doctor's appointments and so on.*

▶▶ *Set strict timings for studies, playtimes and using gadget time with rewards when a job is completed. It need not be completed well, but even if there is sincerity shown to complete, give them that small reward. Rewards encourage them to be better.*

▶▶ *Have one family meal where the conversations are planned on fun and not centred on fault finding or dispute solving time. That can be set aside for a separate time.*

Notes

_____

_____

_____

_____

_____

_____

_____

_____

_____

_____

_____

_____

_____

_____

_____

_____

_____

_____

TEN

Happiness Unleashed

SEEK HAPPINESS AND
IT SHALL BE YOURS

An introduction to 'My Happiness'

You can create happiness from within you to let happiness create a beautiful world for you.

Today countries measure the happiness index. People all around the world recognize the need to be happy. The UN recognizes happiness as a fundamental goal and measures it in terms of social progress, the GDP and life-health index, as a combination of these. World Happiness Day is celebrated on the 20th of March each year. Norway was voted the number one happy country in 2017. China has been at the same level of happiness 25 years ago as it is now in spite of its economic progress. According to research conducted by Richard A. Easterlin, happiness has declined in the USA over the last 10 years. In both China and the United States countries, the decline of social support could be a major contributing factor.

Bhutan was voted one of the happiest Asian countries 10 years ago, even while being economically poor and having a high rate of illiteracy. Money cannot buy happiness. It requires a good and positive state of mind. Today, more and more countries are taking happiness very seriously. The United Arab Emirates has a Ministry for Happiness and the United Kingdom has a Ministry for Loneliness. Both focussing on how to make its population happier.

According to Susan Pinker, a psychologist and social scientist, the top two reasons for people to live long are not clean air or being fit, but it is close relationships and social integration. Longevity can be predicted by how you interact not only with your loved ones, but also socially, how many friends you have and so on. Do you meet your friends regularly for coffee or watch a movie together? Or a game of poker perhaps? Do you say hello to the people in the lift or have a friendly chat with your regular milkman or grocer? These are the things that will make you happy and give you that long, healthy life.

Lots of recent studies on happiness show that it leads to more satisfaction, productivity and success in life. Happiness and not monetary benefit is a key factor to an employee retaining his or her job. Happiness has an impact on your immune system and as a result you can live a long, healthy life. Your surroundings, some meaningful or even random events around you can make you happy. A surprising fact is that you do not need an event to feel happy. You can laugh without a reason and your brain thinks you're happy and releases hormones like endorphins, dopamine and serotonin that make you feel happy with biochemical processes that happen in your body.

Exercise also releases similar happy hormones in your system. Regular exercise keeps a ready stock of these chemicals in your brain and you are able to sustain the feeling of happiness and feeling healthy too. It also reduces the feeling of pain.

Happiness leads to more peaceful sleep and less chances of depression. It reduces incidents of heart diseases or cardiovascular diseases and promotes better health. Being happy is the key to a long-lasting relationship. Happiness can be created irrespective of the situation, by just being positive, through exercise, practicing breathing and simply by practicing the facial expression of a smile.

Happiness makes you think positively. Thinking positively increases the probability of making your thoughts into a reality and of it happening as an event in the future. What we focus on more is what we get more often than not. There was a study of nuns with literally the same lifestyle conditions in Milwaukee in the year 1903, called the Diary of Notre Dame. The nuns who were positive lived 9 years longer than the nuns who had a negative attitude.

Richard J. Davidson, a neuroscientist and professor at the University of Wisconsin, Madison, found that training your brain to be mindful for two weeks, 30 minutes every day, raises your level of happiness. Everything you have learned about the brain suggests that happiness is no different than learning to play a violin or learning to engage in a complex sport. If you practice it, you get better at it, says Davidson. So, happiness is a choice, not a result.

The results of unhappiness manifested as illness

"Nothing can make you happy until you choose to be happy. Your happiness will not come with you, it will only come from you", said Ralph Halson. It is not easy to be happy all the time, I agree. People get consumed by what happens around them. There is no time to be in choice. Stress, anxiety and unhappiness cause deep harm. It disturbs you physically and emotionally. You go deeper in the negative thoughts. These negative thoughts are like bees attracted to honey, except that there's nothing sweet about it. Once unhappy, you cannot be focussed or think straight. You may make wrong decisions. You live life like a burden without any joy. This has a major impact on your physical body. Your immune system becomes weaker and you succumb more easily to common colds or an infection floating around. You'll be the first one to get the bug.

Even infants are sensitive to their surroundings and crave for favorable attention to feel secure and happy. Edward Thornick studies short three-minute interactions of infants with parents. If the parent is inattentive, the infant tends to withdraw, grow weary and turns its face away.

The impact of stress and general unhappy feelings shows up as physical symptoms and ailments in your body, like weight gain, lethargy, lifestyle diseases such as type 2 diabetes, high blood pressure, cardiovascular disease, PCOD and menstruation related issues in women, many of which are reversible. Sometimes you can get small, niggling pains in your body that are totally unexpected, and you can spend time and money trying to find the cause or a cure for that problem unsuccessfully. Unhappiness leads to autoimmune diseases like multiple sclerosis, breathing problems like asthma, food allergies and intolerances, fibromyalgia, rheumatoid arthritis and even some forms of cancer.

This makes you even more unhappy, unable to contribute positively at work or to society or at home. Your relationships towards your spouse, your children or your friends suffers. It makes you frustrated and angry. Anger releases hormones like adrenaline and cortisol, which take up so much of your energy in an unproductive manner. It also creates eating disorders and you can end up losing a lot of weight. Your sleep patterns get disturbed. It negatively impacts your self-image and confidence and your ability to be productive in your personal and professional life.

Some ways to practice happiness

Try learning to dance, sing or even do some gardening. You do not have to be an expert at it, but it lifts your spirit and spreads the infectious happy mood to everyone around you. Happiness is a state of mind. Since your mind and body are connected, you can create your happiness making use of both of them. You can practice laughter therapy and create happiness. Or create a positive attitude and a happy frame of mind that is capable of producing creative ways of dealing with your problems in life. You become in control of your life.

Have you heard of Paul the Octopus predicting the 2010 FIFA World Cup winner? People all over the world were intrigued whether Paul the Octopus understood FIFA or its role in choosing the winner. You will never know. You can call it rubbish and illogical. That will be the thinking mind talking to you. But Paul provided a feeling of fun and curiosity to the game. Have positive thoughts. You are what you think. Albert Einstein's theory of relativity shows that energy and matter are interconvertible. If you sow positive thoughts/energy, you will reap positive actions/matter. The future is all about the unknown. Do all that you can and give it your best and why not be positive about the results?

When you have a problem, share it with trusted family members or friends. It may not offer you a solution, but it may take a load off your shoulders and give you some relief. That window of clear mind may help you come up with or create an answer for your problems.

From the time of cavemen to now, your brains are instinctively trained to be in a protective mode with certain stimuli. It means the moment you perceive anything as a threat, a physical threat or even if it is an emotional one or even an imaginary one, you instinctively react to it, with the intent to protect yourself. You could face the situation aggressively or you could run away and not face it or pretend it does not exist. This protective mechanism is a useful tool to protect you from the perceived dangers and threats. For example, if there is some sound and you feel there could be a burglar in your house, your instinctive reaction will be to lock the doors, try to take a peek outside to verify and maybe call the police. Your heart rate goes up, and this makes your reactions faster. You may not really sit and analyze at this point, if the noise is from a burglar or a friendly neighbor. Your brain does not entertain such thoughts in such situations. Or if you are going to school and the teacher announces a surprise test. You will have a similar reaction, of anxiety. This anxiety may lead to you blanking out on some answers, which you had prepared for so well. Even when your mobile phone falls on the ground and breaks, your brain reads it as a stressful situation and goes into protective mode. You panic, wondering how you will manage your time. Once you gather yourself, you know that your details are stored in the cloud and it may take some time and money, and is an inconvenient situation, but it's nothing that you cannot handle.

These days, you react to any situation with stress. It may be in the office, at home or even something as small as your smart phone's dying battery can trigger a stress reaction in you. This puts your system in a constant "protective mode", with the fight or flight impulse coming into play more often than not. Your brain cannot distinguish what is an actually dangerous situation and what is a perceived one. The body's pulse rate goes up in both situations and the brain reacts in a similar manner. At this time, the analytical part of the brain is not accessible to you.

Studies have shown that people tend to be attracted more to bad news than good news. You are strongly influenced by the happenings in the world around you as portrayed by the media. You come home after a stressful day of work, negotiating your way in traffic, and you switch on the television. What do you see? The media offers news channels highlighting negative news, the programs are more focussed on jealousy, deceit and revenge. There are not many pure entertainment channels focussed on just plain fun. Such stimulus makes you less inclined to be naturally happy and more inclined be more stressed.

When you look at the starry sky at night, you see sparkling specks. When you were told they are stars and planets, you start to make the distinctions. Now if someone were to point out the constellations, your distinctions get further sharp when you look at the night sky. Similarly, in life, distinctions are a useful tool to help you stay grounded and in control. You recognize what causes stress, you make a distinction of what your assessments are about stress and happiness. Being curious and asking "what" questions help you getting clarity. What made you upset and lose your temper the other day? What support do you need in this relationship, that you have not discussed? What is your mood when you are in the sales meeting and what is the one thing that you could do to change in the meeting?

A recent study of a group of people showed that only 13% of people were happy at work. Those who were happy were twice as more productive as their unhappy counterparts. The good news is that happiness is produced in your body and does not always need a reason attached to it. It can simply be produced by smiling. Just smile, laugh and giggle. You don't need a reason to laugh. Look at the children in the park. Hear their laughter. You can feel their happiness. Happiness can also be produced by the feeling of being grateful. Practice gratitude for all things big and small. Be grateful that you can see this beautiful world around you. Be grateful for the love and support of family and friends. Just be grateful to be alive. The process of looking for gratitude is more important than why you are grateful. Verbalizing or journaling your daily gratitude releases happiness hormones into your blood. Hormones such as dopamine and serotonin help reduce anxiety and help you feel happy.

Having emotional agility helps you be happy. This is the ability to move in and out of emotions and not let yourself get drained by your emotions. Exercising also helps the body release happiness chemicals. Being positive and non-judgmental adds an element of lightness in your life. Managing your life in an organized manner and grooming yourself well gives a vibe of confidence and goes a long way to reducing stress. All of these tools make it more probable for you to laugh more and be light in life.

Questions to ask about happiness:

What if you lost your job. How can you be happy?

Yes, you cannot be happy when you lose your job, especially if you have financial burdens amongst other things. But at least you can use this opportunity to take a forced break. It gives you a chance to think about what went wrong and what you can do to prevent it from happening again. You can also think of it as a chance to start afresh, or a career change, or a better opportunity. Being sad is not going to make it any better, so why not try smiling and looking at it from a positive perspective.

What if you just lost your loved one, how can you ever be happy?

Give yourself time to grieve. It takes time and it is not easy to lose someone. One is never prepared for something like this when it actually takes place, but life goes on. Stop playing the blame game or isolating or blocking yourself. Take the help of friends to talk about it and about how you feel.

Some countries have bereavement centres to help you cope and they give you help in legal, financial and other matters too. Once you are ready, use the opportunity to reinvent yourself, while still fondly holding on to some sweet memories. This positive outlook will help in creating lost happiness.

What if you are moving houses and your children are so unhappy?

Any change is difficult. Moving to a new house is a big change and one that is not easy for adults and it is especially more difficult for children. They have to make new friends, be accepted in new groups, maybe even change schools. These are big issues for them. Make them a part of the preparation and make it fun. Take them to the new area before shifting, visiting the neighborhood, giving small treats to the neighborhood children. Make them help you pack. They can make color coded and different designer labels for boxes and for different rooms. They can even choose the color and decor of their room. This inclusive and fun exercise makes it less intimidating an experience.

Action Steps

- *Join or create a laughter club in your area where all one has to do is laugh out loud.*

- *Plan regular meals with friends and family where you play board games, card games or have a karaoke session that involves interactive teamwork and thinking skills. It elevates the total energy of the people.*

- *Get or adopt a pet like a dog or a cat. Pet cuddles release oxytocin, the cuddle hormone in your system, making you feel the love and bond with the pet. It gives a general feel-good, happy energy. Pets sense your emotions and help you overcome the negative feeling of sadness with their warmth, cuddles and unconditional love that makes you want to smile.*

Notes

ELEVEN

Finding the Balance

Mindfulness mantra

What is this mindfulness that everyone talks about? It seems to be the new "mantra". Will it help in finding the balance?

Mindfulness is a process of calming your mind and shifting your attention, thoughts and sensation to this moment, the present. Every time you think of the past or the future, just being aware of it and bringing your mind back to the present again and again, not being judgemental of the thoughts that pass your mind, just to observe and be.

Mindfulness has been practiced in various forms, right from 1500 BC. Be it in Hinduism, Buddhism, Christianity, Muslim and Jewish cultures and others. Mindfulness and stillness lead you to a peaceful mind and a balanced life.

Good things don't come easy. You have worked all your lives forming habits. These habits may have served you in the past. For example, if you're working hard, aggressive and pushing your way with so much competition around you, you do become achievers. But the question to be asked is, are you happy and free of stress? Is this what you want from life? What can you change now to get a life that's peaceful and within your control? Training your brain and mind to relax will enable you to take control, rather than the mind controlling your life.

You have on an average upto 50,000 thoughts in a day. Neuroscientists have shown 95% of your thoughts are in the subconscious mind and just 5% of them are focussed on the conscious present moment. Most of your thoughts are focussed on judging, analyzing, doubting, and reliving your worry again and again. You are not even aware of it most of the time.

Dr. Bruce Lipton, an American development biologist studied epigenetics and says you live most of your life unconsciously, manipulated by your negative thoughts.

Becoming aware, and staying positive and staying in the moment, can change your health and your life in a positive way.

It is all about creating new habits and repeating them again and again and again until you become perfect in this new habit and that's how you start operating.

My husband Ramesh decided that this year he will focus on mindfulness and balance. He wanted to let go of being judgemental. He came up with this great idea of cooking. His cooking skills at the time were limited to making eggs for breakfast. That did not stop him from being curious and wanting to learn this new skill.

What I learned from him is that despite being in a high powered job, he decided to make time for his passion. He was determined. He did not think cooking was a lesser choice to make. He joined a cooking class and served his first cooked meal to his children, their spouses and me. He told me that cooking, right from cutting the vegetables to plating the meal, is all about the balance. Cooking teaches him to balance the colors of the food, the salt with the sweet and the spice, to balance the texture and to focus on the moment. Then the outcome is automatically guaranteed to be a tasty meal. This balance helped him to a great extent on how he showed up in his professional life. This was a great learning for me as well.

Focus on the method, not the outcome

Instead of focussing on the outcome, which one generally tends to do, focus on the method. Usually you focus on what you need. I need money, I need the dress, I need this, I need that. Instead, focus on what you are doing, focus on the moment. Focus on your passion. Don't worry about whether it will work or not, whether it will be successful or not, whether it will make money or not. Those outcomes will come automatically once you follow your passion with a lot of mindfulness.

Mindfulness increases the flexibility to think, act and feel and you start concentrating and getting better results. It improves concentration and your mental clarity, your ability to focus and your cognitive skills to think. This increases the rate of success at work, in academics for children, and at home.

The stress disappears and soon you find that you are more in control of your life. This improves relationships making them better. It also increases self-confidence, your body's immunity, while lowering the risk of and helping to check diseases such as hypertension and type 2 diabetes. It reduces irritability and increases the quality of sleep. It also increases our ability to empathize and be compassionate.

Did you know that after an 8-week practice of mindfulness, the amygdala part of the brain, which is in charge of the stress response, decreases in size? This enables the other parts of the brain, especially those responsible for concentration, focus and awareness, to strengthen and you achieve balanced decision making. This is something that can clearly be seen on before and after MRI scans.

"The little things, the little moments, they aren't little", said Jon Kabat- Zinn, the founder of the Centre of Mindfulness at the University of Massachusetts Medical School.

Your reactions are limited by your mind and your body

When you are stressed, your body may think it is under attack and it takes away your ability to think clearly. This is not a good problem solving strategy. You cannot focus on the real issue and often smaller or less important issues become your point of attention.

Your reactions are not only limited by your mind, but they affect your body as well. Your heart rate increases, your immunity decreases, making you more prone to illness and diseases from common cold to type 2 diabetes, to heart related issues.

Most of these ailments are reversible by reducing stress. With stress you get irritated more easily and this affects your relationship at home and in the office. This in turn shows in your output, reducing the rate of success in your professional life. Even more concerning, is the negative effect on your appetite, sleep and the performance of not only adults, but also children, whose academic results are then affected. Your social life also suffers. Your self-esteem drops, you are always on the edge, you lose your capacity to love and be loved. You become harsh and rude in your mannerisms.

"Life is like riding a bicycle. To keep the balance, you must keep moving", according to Albert Einstein. Training your brain and mind to be still and mindful can be done and achieved by anyone. You don't have to be religious or spiritually oriented for that. They are important tools to achieve peace. Breathing and meditation are useful practices in this regard. Even the basic form of breathing and meditation helps to train the mind to achieve peace.

As discussed earlier, people generally breathe in and out, from and through just below their nostrils and the breath doesn't even reach their throat. Their breathing is shallow. Taking deep breaths from the nostrils, breathing all the way in and expanding your stomach and expanding your chest is the way to do it. Then you slowly release the breath as you empty and contract your stomach. It is a useful breathing practice and you can do this while seated or standing and even while walking or driving. Just be aware of your breath and if it is shallow, start breathing a little deeper. Inhaling deeply makes you aware of the things around you and helps your brain learn.

Whereas, when stressed, you literally stop breathing and hence do not even notice the things around you. When you stop breathing, you stop learning. Believe in the power of positive thinking. In this book, *Breaking the habit of being yourself, how to lose your mind and create a new one*, Dr. Joe Dispensa talks about Einstein's theory of matter and energy and further tells us that a thought or an energy plants a possibility of matter or an event manifesting in the future.

Practicing meditation helps to remove doubts

Thinking positive creates the possibility of the thought becoming a reality in a positive way in the future. It creates a positive energy that will attract other positive thoughts and actions and people and events to you.

There can be no space for even a percent of doubt if you want this to work. I started practicing meditation a few years back, which was basically to breathe sitting in one place. I thought 15 minutes for the first day is a good time, so I sat and into my first breath, I was itching and so I readjusted my seating. I managed a few breaths and then the thought, *"Did I send that important e-mail?"* crossed my mind. I got up to check.

After a few minutes, I noticed my eyes were shut so tight I had to open them. Then I started getting new and creative ideas about my work so I to get up and scribble the points down. It was the longest 15 minutes ever. I guess I had missed the point. Did I feel peace? In fact, I was so irritated and angry with myself. Working on the new habits takes constant practice for at least 3 weeks to 3 months. It is okay to make mistakes and go back to the old ways of thinking and being. Noticing that you have gone back to your old ways is good enough to start the journey of change. There's no need to punish yourself for not adhering to practice at times. This observation is a good mindful exercise, just noticing how you react to the things around you and noticing how the practices help in your transformation. Soon in a matter of days and weeks you will have shifted to the new way of being.

Life is full of stress and anxious moments. You rarely find time to do something about it. But more often than not, taking a few minutes of your precious time, to bring your attention to yourself, gives you a relaxing and positive feeling.

Grounding yourself regularly and how to do it

Walking bare foot in grass is an excellent way to ground yourself. Enjoy the relaxed feeling and enjoy nature. Enjoy the color and smell of the grass, feel the moment of peace it gives your mind. This is a good grounding exercise. Just like electric wires are earthed to remove excessive negative energy, similarly, the feeling of the grass and earth below your feet is totally relaxing. Being with nature immediately sends a relaxing signal to your brain. If you are stressed and have an opportunity to access a garden or grassy area this mindful exercise is an excellent way to connect to your body. Infact, anything that connects your attention to nature helps you ground yourself. Observe the colors of the sky, the sunset and twilight sky, the sky strewn with twinkling stars, observe the flowers around and their colors and fragrance. Observe the birds and try to distinguish the different species by listening to their singing. Observe the waves of the sea and their salty smell. Observe the hills, the snow and the fall colors. Anything that brings you closer to nature helps you connect with yourself.

Becoming grounded to your emotions

Do you know how many human emotions there are? Our social system is not tuned into recognizing the importance of being in touch with your emotions. Just recognizing them and verbalizing them gives a lot of validity and even relief. Acceptance is the first step.

Some human emotions, in no particular order are: Anger, fear, happiness, joy, shame, contempt, surprise, caring, depression, disgust, hurt, confusion, guilt, loneliness, grief, empathy, lust, jealousy, confidence, relief, love, pity, sleepiness, tiredness, irritation, pity, misery, helplessness, hungriness and feeling stupid.

Keeping a journal of your feelings is a useful tool, especially to keep track of your negative emotions. Negative emotions are attracted to you like bees to honey. It is a natural process. It is fine to be sad and cry, and to be happy and laugh out loud. You can express your emotions in a way that does not hurt you or others around you. What if you are angry? Would that mean you can go yelling and throwing things around? While it is good to be in tune with and noticing that you are angry, what helps is trying to observe what is causing the anger. How you can express it in a positive way, by sharing what you feel with the other person, asking for and considering the other person's point of view.

Doing this allows you to be conscious of your general attitude and mood. Many times, when you are angry, you think you are angry, but you may actually be sad deep down. The suppressed and unexpressed sadness comes out as anger, and you believe anger is your default emotion. Similarly, some people love to clown around and may come out as fun people. They may be hiding a lot of sadness under that smiley face. Being curious of your emotions helps you connect with them and with yourself.

Sit on the floor, with your back straight, shoulders stretched out but relaxed, and eyes closed, and start noticing your breath. Do not stop the thoughts that come to you. Notice them and let them be. There is no need to process them. Then continue to focus on your breath. This is a good mindfulness exercise.

Mentally visualizing helps you calm your mind, as long as it is mindful and not a way to escape. I go into my own imaginary garden to feel a relaxed energy. Thinking positive and feeling positive, and believing in it helps you move forward with an open mind and the change of achieving your goals becomes high.

Physical activities like running, gym, yoga, swimming, and playing games like tennis and football, expend all the unused negative energy, releases positive chemicals in your body and make you think fresh. Singing and dancing are also very relaxing. The power of healing through vibration is known from ancient times. It restores an energy equilibrium in your system. Vibrational energy through chanting, music, rhythm and dance is known to having healing properties, healing both physically and mentally. Humans can hear between the frequencies of 20 to 20,000 Hertz. Interacting with dolphins is known to have a calming effect, as dolphins talk in favorable high frequency sounds, inaudible to humans.

Respecting and loving yourself, respecting and loving life are true gifts you can give yourself to help you look inward to tap the powerhouse of positive energy within you.

Questions to ask about concentration practices:

What if you cannot concentrate and sit still?

The point is to just observe your breathing and not stress about whether you're doing it right or wrong. Notice if the breathing gets shallow and correct it.

Where is the time for these practices? You are already so busy and stressed, this will stress you more.

For breathing, like I mentioned, you can practice it literally anywhere, anytime. While having a bath, on your way to work, while driving the car or in a bus, or even in your place of work or in a mall. No one but you will even notice what you are doing.

How can you be positive if all these negative things happened around you? Your colleagues get the promotion you worked so hard for, your mother falls sick when you have this important meeting... all these things happen only to you. You feel the suggestions given are not practical.

The point to focus on is if you continue doing what you're doing, will things get better? So, are your habits and thoughts aiding you to a productive life? If not, it is a good time to introspect. This is when the mindfulness comes to play.

If you add a positive vision of what or where you want to be and believe it from your heart, there is no harm to then checking its results. Life is cyclical. Nobody stays in misery for their entire life, but you can be pessimistic and lose those lovely moments of today in your life. How you create your future depends on your present irrespective of your surroundings.

"No one is stressful, it is your inability to manage your body, mind and emotions that makes you stressed", says Sadhguru Juggi Vasudev.

Action Steps

▶▶ *Spend 5 to 10 minutes in the morning as soon as you wake up and 5 to 10 minutes before you go to sleep practicing deep breathing. You can add to this practice as many times as you want each day.*

▶▶ *Yoga is an excellent mind-body workout. Sun salutation is a 12-step complete body workout. When combined with proper breathing in each step, you focus on your balance, flexibility and stability with body and mind.*

▶▶ *Practice gratitude. Every night before you sleep, along with breathing, say a mental thank you to your family, your mother, your friends and even to nature for being beautiful and serving you. Be grateful to the farmer, the fruits and the person who cooked your yummy food today. To the person who opened the elevator door for you. Just being grateful helps change chemicals in your brain and improves your wellness factor. It helps you be grounded and in balance.*

Notes

TWELVE

Yin Perspective

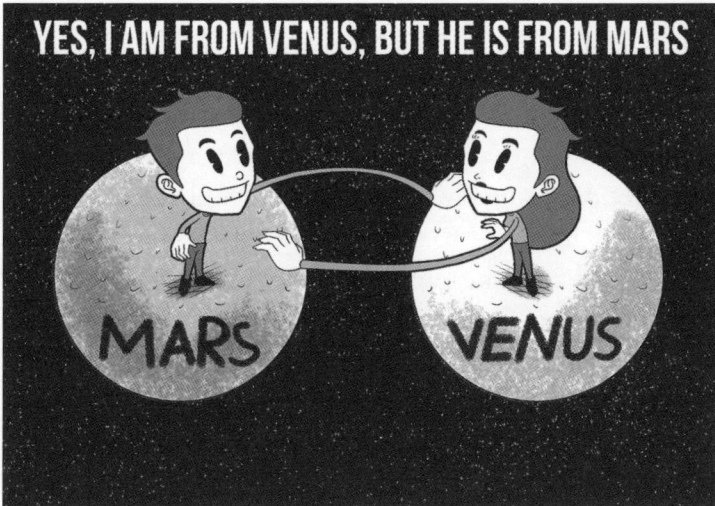

YES, I AM FROM VENUS, BUT HE IS FROM MARS

MARS VENUS

Yin or Yang, who is better?

Women and men have different abilities. Comparing them in some ways is like comparing oranges with apples. They are the same species, yet so different. Calling them equal in some ways is a flawed statement. They can beautifully complement one another and that is the beauty of nature.

Yin and Yang energies are based on an eastern philosophy that says that together they represent harmony. Yin is the slow, intuitive, quite feminine energy and Yang is the active, analytical, forceful masculine energy. Yin-Yang together can be called a paradox. You are not always Yin, soft and flowing, you are not always Yang, aggressive and strong. You are strong and weak at different times, trying to get the balance. Life offers this apparent duality, and when you live without judgements, you appreciate the perfect oneness.

Women and men are different, in looks and in their brain composition. Men want short explanations and to simply choose between A and B, period. Men can narrow their focus and not get distracted by unnecessary information. Men decide rationally, and they are naturally aggressive, genetically modified to hunt and be providers and have a higher level of testosterone. On the other hand, women want big explanations, more options with different permutations and combinations, want to touch and feel things and at the end of it all, they may still not make a decision. Women want to see the big picture. They think and decide emotionally. This explanation is just a broad picture for a general understanding and may or may not be true on an individual level.

Men tend to be physically stronger, and women emotionally stronger. I believe every man has some womanliness in them and every woman has some manliness in them. Some of these opposing characters become obvious when put to test or out of necessity. This does not take away their drive to be achievers.

This world produces amazing and successful women in professional fields, ranging from political leaders, scientists, medical doctors, astronauts, CEOs, entrepreneurs and thousands of successful women in the smaller areas of work, who are equally resourceful. Some of them inspite of the lack of support and education are powerful home makers and nurture their family to success.

Women have much more complex roles to handle than men in my assessment. They juggle multiple roles of daughter, mother, mother-in-law, aunt, home maker, wife, employee, boss, entrepreneur and more.

It is not a competition with the men. Women are just different. Better in some areas than men, whereas men are better in some other areas. Seeing them both in the right perspective gives one the ability to use both these energies to the fullest.

Women have better communicative skills. Women have more vocabulary and are better at using it too. Women speak about 20,000 words per day, 7,000 more words than an average man. The communicative skills make women more articulate and lend clarity to the situation.

The likelihood of a job being complete in time and with perfection, when a woman is involved is higher, the emphasis being on detailing and perfection. This is a useful career tool to possess. Women are better at recalling things, also giving them the benefit of a better memory. Especially useful when it comes to recalling dates in a relationship, men beware.

Memory is an apt skill to have in high level business discussions when you may not have the time to keep referring and need to rely on your memory for important facts, figures and details of contracts being discussed.

Women are more intuitive by nature. The article titled *Intuition Is An Essential Leadership Tool* by Bonnie Marcus featured in the Sept 2015 issue of Forbes focuses on the effectiveness of the intuitive skills of women. Decision making sometimes need to be done on the spur of the moment. Historically, it is not true that a theoretically perfect deal succeeds. You need to rely on your emotional and intuitive side to make that decision and make it a success. Women are good at multitasking. You can multitask efficiently, as long as you use different parts of your brain at one time.

Listening to audio books while walking is a perfect example. Women are better at multitasking effectively and is true also due to their hormones. Estrogen, for example, helps you walk and talk at the same time, a task which men can find difficult and daunting.

Women can switch attention between tasks more easily than men. We have a perfectly rational reason to get irrational once a month. Jokes apart, the menstrual cycle causes the heartbeat to go faster in the second half of the cycle. It makes the woman's heart stronger and healthier, in general, as compared to men. They are also less likely to accumulate belly fat.

"We have to reshape our own perspective of how we view ourselves", says Beyoncé. Unless you have a strong image of yourself, how can you expect others to have that image of you?

Women are women's worst enemy at times. Women bow to pressures of the culture and the society and unconsciously accept men as being superior to women. They may be mistaking the physical strength of men with the emotional aptitude of women as a weakness.

I have heard mothers tell daughters to "adjust" in a marriage. I've seen women accepting without a fight when men get promoted over them in their career, despite them being a better candidate. If the children start to stray, the women almost take it upon themselves and feel guilty and think they cannot contribute equally to home and at work. There are no perfect mothers. So why punish yourself with the guilt?

Women are prone to sexual harassment. 75% of the cases are not even reported. A recent study shows that 75% of those cases that are reported, go against women. I admire the recent move, #metoo, an initiative that started in October 2017 after the infamous case involving a Hollywood personality came to light. To come out in the open and to share the pain of harassment, that is a woman's power.

As a woman, the likely energy is of a nurturer, a provider and is emotionally oriented. We have the power to give birth to our children. While this is a beautiful gift, it does not come without pain. There are times when the child needs the mother more than the father. Making smart and value-based choices helps, but as always, to get something, you need to choose and prioritize. Plan your pregnancy, divide some child rearing and housekeeping tasks with your spouse. Outsourcing some tasks without the feeling of guilt can make this period the best one in your life.

"When looking for a life partner, my advice to women is to date all kinds of them. The bad boys, the good boys, the committed phobic boys, the crazy boys. But do not marry them. The things that make the bad boys sexy do not make them good husbands. When it comes to settling down, find someone who wants to be an equal partner, someone who thinks women should be smart, opinionated and ambitious, someone who values fairness or expects, even better, wants to do his share in the home. These men exist and trust me, over time nothing is sexier", says Sheryl Sandberg, the COO of Facebook.

The flexibility of Yin energy

Yin energy is all about flexibility and space. It's about being and allowing others to be. Believe in yourself and respect yourself, if you want others to believe in you and respect you. Women being more emotional and nurturing by nature, tend to give themselves the least amount of time and priority. How can you be good at serving others when you're tired and emotionally drained and unhappy?

Give yourself that extra time and treat yourself to a spa date. It is ironic, but if you eat first you are stronger and better able to feed your children, rather than tending to your children first when you're so hungry, leading to frustration, anger and irritation.

Learn to say "No". You don't have to offend anyone. You will realize that people more often than not accept a sweet no with a good reason. It shows them that you value yourself enough not to take on more than what you think you can deliver.

There are certain things that men can do better; accept them and use them to your advantage. If your car broke down, maybe you can replace a tire, no big deal. I believe recognizing your strengths and weaknesses is far more valuable and useful to help you be efficient in what you choose to do. Choose wisely.

Ontological coaching and its uses

What is ontological coaching? What is coaching? Who will benefit from coaching, especially ontological coaching?

You learn through your experiences. You judge events based on your experiences. You judge people based on your intelligence and your experiences. Your experiences allow you to form a perception. Your perception of what you think is a fact or is true. You make your set of assumptions of this world based on your personal experiences. Based on these assessments, you develop behaviors. Over time you develop some habits, and you become good at them and they become so obvious, that you miss noticing them. When it is not useful and comes in the way of achieving your potential, a coach or a guide helps you discover these habits and allows you to be in choice to change. Coaching helps you shift from knowledge to wisdom.

When people are confused or stressed in life or have a mental need or seek some guidance in a particular aspect in life, they may choose to get professional help. They can go to a psychologist. They are especially skilled at dealing with some forms of mental illness such as depression, sleeping disorders and learning disabilities. Some mental illnesses need the care of a psychiatrist. A counsellor can work with an individual or a family or a group of people and is skilled at dealing with relationship issues, maybe in an office, marriage or with your children, amongst other things. They use therapy and provide answers to the problem in hand. There are many other types of healers and therapists as well.

When you are confused or stuck in life and need a sounding board or a mirror, and if you want to be better in what you do and take it to the next level of efficiency and productivity, an ontological coach is a good fit. Just like you need a coach to be better in golf or tennis. In life a coach helps you introspect and leads you to a path of discovery.

What is right and what is wrong? There is no right and wrong or good or bad. Ontological coaching is a philosophical way of looking at life and its problems. Life is an experience. You make mistakes and learn from them. This gives you an opportunity to do things differently. If the new way of doing or being also does not work, then at least you will know that and you have tried it out. You will then try another way of doing or being.

Ontological coaching does not offer readymade solutions. The coach is like a mirror, a reflecting board for you. The coach offers their undivided attention, is a good listener and is curious and will ask you a lot of reflective questions. The coach helps you shift in the way you see things and offers many scientifically researched techniques to sustain the shift and new way of being. The coach helps draw the attention to your habits, especially the ineffective ones.

Being reflective helps you come up with alternate solutions for your issues. The brain has formed strong neural connections with the old habits. It is not easy to form and practice new habits. Only knowing is not enough. It requires will power and determination to practice, practice, and practice to form the new habits. Ontological coaching is an art and a science thrown into one.

Ontological coaching is a useful approach that helps all those people who are either stuck in life, stuck at work and cannot see growth, or are just curious about life or this coaching in general. It works to shift your way of being and opens up a lot of possibilities to a new You, allows you to achieve your goals in happiness, lightness and offers a good balance in your life.

The new way of being and new habits are often focussed on looking inwards. You are trained by default to be clinical and logical and a thinking being. Society does not greatly encourage exploring the creative and 'feeling' side of people. Believing in magic is almost frowned upon. This pattern of thinking is constantly enforced by the schools, your parents and society. An equal part of you is also a feeling being. Focussing on thinking and feeling together is a great way to being balanced. Ontological coaching techniques involve the body or somatic, language and emotions to enable to be a complete human being.

Somatic exercises like mindful breathing, dance and music help focus your attention to the moment. The way you hold your body allows you to alter your thinking and the way you act. If you round your shoulders inward and stoop forward, folding both your arms, it does not give the perception of a confident person. To appear confident, you can broaden your shoulders and relax, open your chest wide and relax both your hands. If you want to have a flexible attitude, dancing is a good practice to adopt.

When you use words, they generate different reactions in people. You can phrase your sentences to be mindful of other people's feelings. I can tell my friend that her choice of clothes is horrible and makes her look fat. Do you think she will appreciate my good intent? I can rephrase it and tell her that some dress brings out her chirpy character and point it out to her. Soon I could be having a conversation with her, as she will be more accepting of my views.

The use of emotions in ontological coaching is a valuable tool. It is the one I struggled with the most. I had built this story in my head, where I saw myself as analytical, logical and structured. When I encountered anything other than this way of thinking, I used to get thrown off track. It used to disturb me. For example, if my family had decided we were going for a Chinese meal, and the restaurant was booked, any change to the plan made me upset. I used to internalize my upset. Sometimes no one around would even notice it. The change may have worked out into a better meal, but I was not happy. What did I do about it? Understanding my feelings and learning to verbalize them was a good start. I started being curious. What was my assessment of the situation? What made me feel bad? What was I thinking? Once I started sharing my feelings with my family, flexibility became easy. It changed the way I perceived things around me. I no more restrict myself to being structured and logical. It still forms a good part of me, but I am willing to be open to other feelings and thoughts. It opened up new possibilities in me. Do I still judge people? Yes, I do. Am I perfect? No. I am learning every day of my life. I am becoming a better observer. I try to focus on the moment. I am in choice of what I want to do and what I want to let go. I feel a big shift in my energy to being positive and able to succeed in my goals in balance and happiness.

Questions to ask about managing Yin energy:

What if you have to get your children ready for school before you leave for work? Your husband leaves very early for work. It is not possible for him to help. You are always late, and you are looking at taking a part time home based job. Is that the right solution?

It is easy to make excuses. You need determination with careful planning and division of labor. The children's school bag and clothes can be ready the night before and it can be your husband's part of the house-work. He could wake the children up and leave for work. That makes it easier for you to get them ready.

What if you are constantly harassed by your male colleagues. He is your immediate boss, what can you do?

If you don't fight injustice, a part of you will die. You will then suffer from low self-esteem and feel powerless and lack confidence. Even though statistics do not show cases favoring women in these situations, unless you stand up and inspire more women to stand up for what is right, nothing is going to change. Not in your generation, not in the next generation.

Yes, you may lose your job, you may suffer shame, but it is better than living in fear. At least you have your pride, which will surely get you the job that is right for you.

What if you are having marital issues and you went to your friend for help and advice, and she said all men are the same and you should leave your husband?

Friends are a great help and form a good support system. Asking someone who are themselves going through similar issues that you are going through, but not knowing how to handle the situation, will not be of much help. Their views will definitely be biased. In certain matters, you have to choose wisely. In some cases professional help may make more sense. Use your judgement of what works best for you.

Action Steps

▸▸ *Love your body and be well groomed and wear your attitude. Your body and mind are part of you as a whole. You cannot have an unhealthy body or be careless about the way you dress and expect yourself to be confident and others to respect you.*

▸▸ *Have fun coffee dates with your girlfriends. Bitch about your husband and the whole world. As long as it's an excuse to release your stress, use it in lightness, laugh and have fun.*

▸▸ *If men are from Mars, women are from Venus. Try to look at things from another perspective, before you judge. This will make you appreciate the differences without judgement, and live life in oneness and harmony.*

Notes

Afterward

Congratulations and thank you for taking the time out to read and give this topic your attention. You would have realized by now that reading *The Game of Change* does not bring about The Change. Change is not easy, especially the ones that give the best results. If you are willing to introspect, and observe the patterns and habits within you that are not working in your life, that is the first step to change. You have worked all your life towards unwittingly forming these habits, which you have perfected over the years. They have formed strong neural paths in your brains. Nothing is permanent but change. Try out new habits and ways of living. Choose the ones that work, and work on these new habits, practicing and repeating them again and again till they form the new and defined neural path in the brains, while the old habits fade away.

Go over the different techniques and try out the exercises offered at the end of each chapter that helps you in this change. They are well researched tweaks and tricks that work. Be open, optimistic and pragmatic in your approach to achieve the transformation to a new defined you; the one with the image of yourself that you will love.

Wishing you all the very best in your journey of discovery.

OFFER 1

Interact with
Geeta Ramakrishnan
on her book:
The Game of Change

To book
Geeta Ramakrishnan
as a speaker of an event,
Please email details to
thegameofchange18@gmail.com

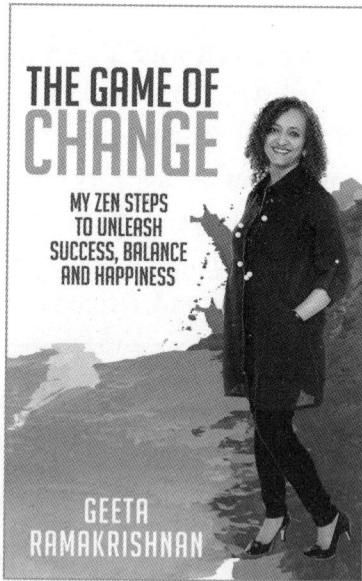

OFFER 2

Be the player in the Game of Change.
Book a 2-day Retreat with
Geeta Ramakrishnan and
Get your downloadable planner
and workbook with easy to follow cheat sheets.

We offer retreats in various parts of the world.
You can also make your own group of
minimum 10 members
to create a custom-made retreat.

For those interested
please email details of your interest
with your name to
thegameofchange18@gmail.com
And we will revert with our schedule.

OFFER 3

Book a trial offer:
Introductory
One on One Ontological Coaching
With **Geeta Ramakrishnan**
(In person or via e-media)

For details
Please email
geeta@coachingwithgeeta.com
www.coachingwithgeeta.com
Your privacy is our top priority

References

Chapter 1

Trust: The Key to Social Harmony, Joe Navarro, October, 2017, Psychology Today, https://www.psychologytoday.com/us/blog/spycatcher/201710/trust-the-key-social-harmony

Chapter 2

The aging mind: neuroplasticityin response to cognitive training, Denise C. Park, March 2013, Dialogues Clin Neuroscience, 15(1): 109-119, https://www.ncbi.nlm.nih.gov/pmc/articles/PMC3622463/

Neuroplasticity: The 10 Fundamentals Of Rewiring Your Brain, Debbie Hampton, reset.me, October, 2015, http://reset.me/story/neuroplasticity-the-10-fundamentals-of-rewiring-your-brain/

Anxiety: When our breathing overreacts in an unbalanced way, Michael Grant White, Breathing.com, http://www.gmhcn.org/files/Wellness/AnxietyFearandBreathing.html

Chapter 4

Paternal Environmental and Lifestyle Factors Influence Epigenetic Inheritance, EstephanyFerrufino,Februrary 2018,What is Epigenetics. com, https://www.whatisepigenetics.com/paternal-environmental-lifestyle-factors-influence-epigenetic-inheritance/

Epigenetics Are Important To Evolutionary Success, January 2013, What Is Epigenetics.com, https://scitechdaily.com/epigenetics-are-important-to-evolutionary-success/

Epigenetics: Fundamentals, What Is Epigenetics.com, https://www.whatisepigenetics.com/fundamentals/

Chapter 5

How Much Time Do People Spend on Social Media?, Evan Asano, Social Media Today, January, 2017, https://www.socialmediatoday.com/marketing/how-much-time-do-people-spend-social-media-infographic

Eisenhower's Urgent/Important Principle, MindTools.com, https://www.mindtools.com/pages/article/newHTE_91.htm

Pressure Doesn't Have to Turn into Stress, Nicholas Petrie, March, 2017, Harvard Business Review,https://hbr.org/2017/03/pressure-doesnt-have-to-turn-into-stress

Chapter 6

If your brain were a computer, how much storage space would it have?, Robbie Gonzalez, Gizmodo.com, May, 2013, https://io9.gizmodo.com/if-your-brain-were-a-computer-how-much-storage-space-w-509687776

The Top 10 Factors For On-The-Job Employee Happiness, Jacob Morgan, December, 2014, Forbes.com,https://www.forbes.com/forbes/welcome/?toURL=https://www.forbes.com/sites/jacobmorgan/2014/12/15/the-top-10-factors-for-on-the-job-employee-happiness/&refURL=https://www.google.ae/&referrer=https://www.google.ae/

Chapter 7

Too Much Emotional Intelligence Is a Bad Thing, AgataBlaszczak-Boxe, March, 2017, Scientific American,https://www.scientificamerican.com/article/too-much-emotional-intelligence-is-a-bad-thing/

Dance your way to happiness, Martha Roberts, August, 2016, Psychologies,https://www.psychologies.co.uk/dance-your-way-happiness

Vibrational Healing, C. G. Harvey & A. Cochrane, HarperCollins, 2017

Chapter 8

Top 10 Reasons Relationships Fail, Preston Ni, July, 2015, Psychology Today, https://www.psychologytoday.com/blog/communication-

success/201507/top-10-reasons-relationships-fail

7 Weird but Scientifically-Proven Ways to Be Happy, Richie Norton, December, 2017, Medium, https://medium.com/the-mission/7-data-driven-happiness-practices-weird-yet-effective-from-science-f34ac20ddabf

How The Cuddle Hormone Could Cure Your Headache, Christine Morgan, November, 2013, Huffington Post, http://www.huffingtonpost. co.uk/2013/11/06/how-the-cuddle-hormone-could-cure-your-headache_n_7413202.html

Emotional Abuse: Definitions, Signs, Symptoms, Examples, May, Natasha Tracy, 2016, Healthy Place.com, https://www.healthyplace.com/ abuse/emotional-psychological-abuse/emotional-abuse-definitions-signs-symptoms-examples/

Chapter 10

The Research: The Still Face Experiment, Michael Fulwiler, March, 2013, The Gottman Institute, https://www.gottman.com/blog/the-research-the-still-face-experiment/

The Economics of Happiness, Richard A. Easterlin, http://www-bcf.usc. edu/~easterl/papers/Happiness.pdf

Why face-to-face contact matters in our digital age, Susan Pinker, March, 2015, The Guardian, https://www.theguardian.com/books/2015/mar/20/ secret-long-happy-life-mountain-villages-sardinia

Counting Blessings Versus Burdens: An Experimental Investigation of Gratitude and Subjective Well-Being in Daily Life, Robert A. Emmons & Michael E. McCulloch, Journal of Personality and Social Psychology, 2003, Vol. 84, No. 2, 377-389http://greatergood.berkeley.edu/pdfs/ GratitudePDFs/6Emmons-BlessingsBurdens.pdf

Chapter 11

3 Facts About Mindfulness,AlefTrust,https://www.aleftrust.org/3-facts-about-mindfulness/

Interesting Facts about Mind and Mindfulness,Aware Meditation App, https://awaremeditationapp.com/interesting-facts-about-mind-and-mindfulness/

It's now a proven fact – Your unconscious mind is running your life!, Life Trainings.com, http://www.lifetrainings.com/Your-unconscious-mind-is-running-you-life.html

How Many Thoughts Does Your Mind Think in One Hour?, Remez Sasson, Success Consciousness, https://www.successconsciousness.com/blog/inner-peace/how-many-thoughts-does-your-mind-think-in-one-hour/

Chapter 12

11 Pros and Cons of Being a Woman, Green Garage Blog.org, https://greengarageblog.org/11-pros-and-cons-of-being-a-woman

24 Unbelievable Facts About Women From Around The World, Rishabh Banerji, May, 2017, India Times, https://www.indiatimes.com/culture/who-we-are/24-unbelievable-facts-about-women-from-around-the-world-230502.html

65 Motivating Quotes From Strong Women We Love ,Style Caster, http://stylecaster.com/beauty/strong-women-quotes/#ixzz54GGZc3Jp

Study finds 75 percent of workplace harassment victims experienced retaliation when they spoke up, Tara Golshan, October, 2017, Vox, https://www.vox.com/identities/2017/10/15/16438750/weinstein-sexual-harassment-facts